From Sixty Two to Sixty Two

Chris Maxwell

From Sixty Two to Sixty Two

CONTENTS

Introduction	2
1 Early Years	3
2 The St. Pat's Years	12
3 The Holy Rosary Years	19
4 The St. Anselm's Years	25
5 High Days and Holidays	29
6 Hobbies and Interests	36
7 Toys, Games and Hanging Out	40
8 Tweens and Teens	47
9 Jobs	55
10 Going Out	58
11 Music and Gigs and TV Shows	61
12 Relatives, Neighbours and Friends	65
13 Places	70
14 The Salford Years	74
15 The Green Goddess and Other Modes of Transport	86
16 Booth Hall – Sick Kids Nursing	89

| 17 | More Holidays and The One That Changed My Life! | 91
| 18 | Early Days in Edinburgh | 94
| 19 | Becoming Mrs Maxwell and a Mum | 101
| 20 | Books and Reading | 105
| 21 | Friends From Near and Far | 109
| 22 | The Teaching Years | 113
| 23 | The ESMS Years | 115
| 24 | Holidays With and Without Children | 119
| 25 | Writing | 124
| Epilogue | 127
| Acknowledgements | 131

To Paul and Suzy so you know where your mum came from!

Introduction

I didn't even know what a memoir was when I started writing this! What I discovered though was that this is not an autobiography as it doesn't span the whole of my life but rather sums up some of what I have done from being born in 1962 to becoming 62 years old. When I started to write this, I quickly realised that until now I had no great interest in my family history and I expect the same will be true for my children. It did become clear though that by the time I was interested and got around to doing something about it many of the people and events were forgotten or unavailable. I hope at some point you find it interesting and at least learn a little of your heritage without having to do too much research yourselves.

1

Early Years

I was born in the Abbey Hills area of Oldham in Lancashire where my mum and dad and four older siblings lived. My dad was William James Fitzsimons, mostly known as Jim, and my mum was Mary Winterbottom.

We lived in a small terraced house, two rooms upstairs, one for the boys, John and Eric and one that mum and dad shared with the girls, Mags and Liz, and two downstairs, a room and kitchen. There was no indoor bathroom and they went down steps at the back of the house to get to the outside toilet. I didn't live there for very long and have no memory of it at all. We moved just around my first birthday to a council estate called Fitton Hill and my mum died shortly after when I was fourteen months old. She had Multiple Sclerosis and bowel cancer which in those days was not really treatable.

Eric, John, Liz and Mags

Me and Liz

On weekdays I lived at my grandparents' home until I was almost seven years old, although my grandad died when I was about three. Liz and I, the younger of my two older sisters, lived there Monday to Friday and went "home" at the weekend. It was an unusual but not unhappy childhood

I was of course oblivious to the trauma of losing a mum, unlike my siblings who were all much more vulnerable ages than I was. Growing up without her certainly had its challenges but unlike my siblings I didn't know any different. I had many "substitute" mums including two big sisters, Mags and Liz, as well as neighbours and friends. They all did their best and as I said, I had a happy if unconventional childhood. Being the youngest, by nine years, I was considered the absolute baby of the family and I know I was very much loved by all. They were of course completely biased but seemed to think I was an exceptionally beautiful baby!

Winning first prize at the Baby Show just reinforced this and I think over the years I've milked it on many occasions. I do still have the certificate to prove it though just in case any of them forget!

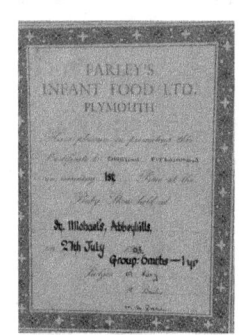

Proof I won the Bonnie Baby Competition

One of my earliest memories is standing outside the front door of gran and grandad's house which was 126 Eldon Street in Oldham, Lancashire. I must have been about three and I was wearing a winter coat and blue mittens. No idea where I was going or why I was standing there but it's very vivid. Grandad was still alive at this point but must have died shortly after. He always used to buy us Maltesers and Five Boys chocolate on pension day. The Five Boys chocolate had five different faces embossed on it ranging from crying to smiling – a bit like emojis of the 60's!

Eldon Street – Our house would have been towards the bottom of the street on the right

The house was a real Coronation Street type house – two up two down, which meant a living room and kitchen downstairs and two bedrooms upstairs. No bathroom, and the toilet was outside in the backyard. We shared the backyard with two other houses but not the toilet, we each had our own. Ours was considered "posh" because it was a regular flush toilet with a chain. The other two were "tipple" toilets and I think they worked with gravity; all I remember of them was they were quite unpleasant. Obviously, if we needed the toilet through the night, it was either a trip outside in the dark and cold or use the "potty" under the bed. Neither was an option unless you were absolutely desperate and I attribute my strong bladder to my early years in Eldon Street and subsequent careers in both nursing and teaching, where going to the loo on demand is not an option!

Having a bath was also an experience although not one I did too often. Mostly I had a bath at home over the weekend as we had the luxury of a bathroom and running hot water. In those days most people didn't bathe every day and almost no one had a shower. On the odd oc-  casion when I bathed at our grandparents' house it was a massive operation to get the tin bath from the back yard where it hung on a nail. It would be set up in front of the fire and pans and kettles full of boiling water poured in. The temperature was never quite right though, and you either got the skin off your bum if it was too hot or a freezing dip in cold water if not. Maybe that's where I get my love of cold water dipping now! Most of the time I was washed in the sink, sitting on the wooden draining board with my feet in the bowl. Gran washed every day after lunch at the sink, and would then put on her "afternoon clothes". On

Oldham Swimming Baths

Friday afternoons though she would go to the "baths" in town. I can't remember how much it cost but on the odd occasions I was allowed to join her I know she was given a towel and a bar of soap and ushered into a room with a single bath. The rooms were partitioned off but had no ceiling so you could hear whoever else was having a bath at the same time.

Bath time was always after she had been to the Tommyfield Market in Oldham.

The market hall was a hive of community activity and there were also the outdoor stalls that sold mostly fruit and veg, cheap shoes and clothing, records and fabric material. The market hall sold cheese and cold meats, biscuits and sweets and ironmongery. There was a café and occasionally I was allowed a glass of sarsaparilla or,

Tommy Field Market

even less frequently, a hot Vimto on a cold day. Gran wasn't given to spending on luxuries and they were definitely classed as luxury.

Dobby Horses at Tommyfield Market

There was also a roundabout or the dobby horses as we called them which was a real treat and only something you got to go on for very special occasions. Sadly, the old indoor market burned down in 1974 and that was the beginning of the end for the market as we knew it.

On the way home we would stop at the "arcade" which was like another indoor street market, albeit much smaller, where some distant relative called George had a biscuit shop. Gran always bought loose biscuits, often broken, because they were cheaper, and sometimes I got a sneaky one from George. My favourite was a pink wafer or a milk biscuit with a picture of a cow on. Then the last stop was John Ash the butcher where she bought a half chicken or half a shoulder of lamb, some beef sausage and bacon. Sometimes lamb's liver, never pork because she said that had caused her to have an ulcer, I'm not sure where she got the idea for that from or why bacon was okay! The worst thing ever though was tripe which she ate cold with vinegar on - yuk. The chicken or lamb was for the weekly roast, cooked and eaten on Saturday, never Sunday. Sunday was for church and not work so she only heated up leftovers, no actual cooking. In fact, she would put the food on a dinner plate on top of a pan of water and leave it simmering until she came back. Only once did I remember the pan being burnt when she got home. If I ever did stay over at her house on a Saturday night, I was always sent to the Catholic church with Auntie Ruth, our next-door neighbour, on Sunday morning. Gran was staunchly Church of England and I think, horrified that my mum had chosen to marry, not only an Irishman, but a Catholic and they had *five* children. Three of whom I'm sure she felt were absolutely surplus to requirements although she loved us all deeply, even me who arrived nine years after my sister and who she had to take care of when she was well into her seventies and eighties.

Every week followed a pattern and there was very little deviation from it. Mondays were washing days. We didn't have a washing machine, so regular clothes were washed by hand in the sink and wrung out using a huge mangle. Sheets and towels were taken up to the launderette but only for washing, they came back wet, went through the mangle to get more excess water out, and then were hung on the line to dry. The sheets were always white cotton and starched to look crisp and clean - hellish on the heels and elbows! Coloured sheets, or heaven forbid, patterned ones, were considered totally unnecessary and quite vulgar!

Mondays were also "tater hash" day - food always had its own day. Tater hash was a cheap and filling type of stew, made of whatever meat was left over after the weekend. It was added to a pot with potatoes, onions, carrots and barley. Dinner was always a meal eaten in the middle of the day and at teatime we had something lighter like eggs or beans on toast. Toast was usually made over the open coal fire and you had to hold the two-pronged fork close enough to toast the bread but not your hand - no health and safety then! We didn't really have snacks, but most days I got an apple or orange mid-morning. Sometimes in season I got to shell peas sitting on the back step and was allowed to eat a few of those. They always came wrapped in newspaper from the market and it seemed like there was a lot until I'd had my share! In rhubarb season, I was given a saucer of sugar and a stick of rhubarb to dip into it. Likewise, pomegranates were another seasonal delight this time with a pin to stab the seeds, looking back, quite exotic!

As I said each day of the week had its own culinary delights, usually based around potatoes in one form or another. They were cheap, filling and helped to bulk out meat which was more expensive. Tuesdays were most often Hot Pot days made with neck of lamb and sliced potatoes, carrots and onions or occasionally "Liver and Onions," not so good! Wednesdays were always "Potato Pie" days followed by apple pie and Carnation cream. Gran made her own pastry for the pies and would often give me a small piece to roll out. Occasionally, she would let me add jam or raisins to it and I was allowed to eat that myself, usually straight from the oven resulting in a burnt tongue. Sometimes, before I started school, my dad would come in his lunch hour on Wednesdays to see me. He and Gran had a distant, polite relationship, sometimes a bit strained. Gran didn't approve of dad going to the pub for a pint and of course I think she had the whole Irish Catholic thing going on. As I say they were polite but there was no real warmth between them. Thursdays were "Cottage Pie" days usually with peas, if I had left enough after shelling and eating most of them! Fridays were glorious "Fish and Chips." When we lived on Eldon Street, I think she bought it from the market but when she moved to North Croft there was a fish van that came round. It was always a small piece of cod that she poached in homemade parsley sauce. Chips were made in the chip pan with beef dripping that she had to melt before frying the chips. Most of the time we had it with peas, we always had vegetables with "dinner," which was at lunchtime before I went to school. I don't remember having anything more exotic than carrots, peas, cauliflower, cabbage and occasionally green beans. I'm sure I never had broccoli until I was an adult. Dad often gave us butter beans and broad beans with our meals at home and the worst thing of all...curried beans. I hated them all but have made friends with butter beans and broad beans as an adult, not so much curried beans!

As young as we were, we all "played out." The street was a hotchpotch of families and you just went outside and joined in with whatever was going on. There were no age restrictions and we seemed to have our own set of rules and regulations. If you were the youngest you were grateful to get a chance to join in and if you didn't, you never said a word. You watched and you waited and eventually at some point, at some time, you might be included. It was never intended or perceived as a form of bullying as it would be in today's world, where everyone has to be included and not left out. You either built up resilience or you got good at the game so you were allowed to play. Eldon Street was the first or last, depending on how you saw it, of three streets running adjacent to each other and parallel to a communal waste ground at the bottom of each street, known affectionately as the "Bottom." It's where you made your way to if there was no one on the street and since there were three streets that led to it there was always someone to play with there. There was a bit of snobbery involved in the streets and we always considered Eldon Street to be unofficially more upmarket. Webster Street running next was ok, but there were some dubious characters living on Falcon Street even rumours of a murder, or so we were told! I never did know if that was true or not.

The railway ran parallel to the Bottom and there were no fences or "Keep Out" signs. We often played around the edges and listened for the train coming before scooting off back onto the relatively safe haven of the Bottom. Health and Safety wasn't something on our minds. Looking back, I'd be horrified if my kids did half of what I did or perhaps if I knew about half of what they did!. We had no watches but were expected to be back at meal times or to come when we were shouted in or when it got dark, and by and large, we did. We came home hungry, dirty and happy. We argued, sometimes fought, and made up games with rules that we stuck to...mostly.

Games came in seasons – skipping rope, where all the girls lined up and took turns to go in the middle to skip to a rhyme that everyone chanted. When the rhyme finished you were out and took your turn at the rope. If you messed up you were out immediately and didn't get to carry on until it was your next turn. There were all sorts of actions that went with the rhymes and they became more complex the better you got at skipping. The best one was when a whole group of girls, always girls, jumped in the rope at the same time. This took coordination, patience, agility and cooperation. The rhyme went:

All in together girls, very fine weather girls,
When I count twenty the rope must be empty.
5, 10, 15, 20

and everyone had to be out without stopping the rope. Then the rhyme continued with:

When I count ten the rope must be full again 5, 10
and everyone had to be back in, jumping in time.

What fun, what skill, and all you needed was someone's washing line. No one said it wasn't fair when they were out, you just waited for your next turn.

Two Ball was another favourite where you juggled two balls alternately against a flat wall and again sang a rhyme. We did all kinds of convoluted actions as we chanted and the idea was to get through as many of them without dropping a ball. My favourite rhyme was:

*Apple, Orange, Banana **peel***
*Fish and Chips will make a **meal***

The actions were carried out on *peel* and *meal* and involved passing the ball under one leg and catching it, slamming a ball sideways against the wall or doing an "uppy." This meant throwing it up in the air mid sequence. We had fantastic hand eye coordination and almost perfect balance. Two Ball could be practised anywhere there was a flat wall and the last house on Eldon Street which belonged to Uncle Bob and Auntie Annie (all neighbours were aunties and uncles out of respect) was the perfect spot. It must have driven them mad to have the constant bouncing of balls against their wall but they rarely complained. Uncle Bob famously woke us all up every morning at 6am as he walked up the street in his metal clogs to go to work. No one needed an alarm clock and no one took offence at the noise. There was a lot of unspoken respect and give and take. As kids, if we hurt ourselves, any number of neighbours would patch us up, wipe our tears and noses and send us on our way. Equally, they would give you a good telling off if they caught you doing something you shouldn't and then you'd be in trouble again once you got found out at home. How times have changed!

2

The St. Pat's Years

So, life was generally happy, daily routines were a comfort and although it wasn't the most conventional of childhoods, it was good. Weekends at home were nothing like weekdays at Gran's but they were ok too, just different. We even had a telly at home, but you had to feed it two-shilling pieces to keep it on and we didn't have many. I do have memories of me and my sisters Mags and Liz being in on Saturday night and watching, what would now be considered, terribly inappropriate programmes like "Till Death us Do Part" with Alf Garnett. I didn't really have much interest in TV to be honest but it was a novelty. We had to make sure there was enough of the two-shillings worth of viewing left for Dad to watch Match of the Day when he came in from the pub! TV in those days went off after News at Ten, I think, and didn't come on again until late afternoon. It wasn't until the early 70's that daytime TV was a thing.

Anyway, life changed when I turned four and a half…I went to school! Until then, apart from weekends, I did everything with my Gran. We went to the park, I "helped" with the housework, played for hours on my own with my dolls and of course I "played out" on the street. I never went to a playgroup or nursery and was never looked after by anyone who wasn't family or a close friend.

Being an August birthday in England meant being the youngest in the year as the cut-off date for school was the end of August. There was the option though for the younger children like me to start at Easter. I didn't have any expectations of school.

St Pat's Primary School

I don't think I even really thought about it, and as far as I remember there were no induction days or pre visits. On my first morning I was taken along to St. Patrick's Infants and Junior School and then realisation dawned...I was to be left!

The head was a nun, an old nun and a no-nonsense nun, called Sister Mary Camillus. She firmly took my hand and led me inside to a classroom full of children, around forty, I think. I wasn't aware if anyone else was new that day but I knew, when they all stood at their desks and joined their hands to pray, that I didn't have a clue what they were saying. In spite of going to Mass every Sunday I didn't know the prayer, Hail Mary. I had no idea what I was supposed to be saying or to bow my head whenever I said Jesus and I was very puzzled by the line

"Blessed is the fruit of thy womb, Jesus."

I remember nothing else of that day, not who I sat with, what happened at playtime and lunchtime, what I did or didn't do. I have no idea what my first teacher was called, she was tall and strict and didn't smile. What I do remember are the terrible temper tantrums I had every day after that first day when it came to going into school. I kicked and screamed and cried and begged and refused to go in. I hated leaving Gran and even at four and half I knew I must be stupid because everyone else could do everything and I couldn't. It took me long into my adulthood to realise they had all been at school for almost eight months when I started and perhaps, I wasn't so "thick" after all.

The tantrums continued daily, apparently it was most of that final term of the school year, which was my first term. I knew I'd gone too far though when I kicked Sister Mary Camillus. She had got into the habit (no pun intended!) of standing in front of me, backing me into the corner of the door. It wasn't meant as a punishment, it was a method of containment as I screamed and cried and tried to escape. One day I went too far and kicked her in the back of her legs. Strangely I have no recollection of what followed, I don't remember receiving any punishment, but even I knew I'd gone too far. After that I succumbed to going into class without a fuss. I hope Sister Camillus felt it was worth a bruised calf in exchange for a bit of peace and quiet. Maybe it wasn't as bad as I felt it had been and maybe if I'd kicked a bit harder, I would have been expelled and that would have been a very satisfactory outcome – if only I'd have thought of that one! There ended the tantrums in school but they re-emerged with a vengeance later at home!

School became much more bearable, even fun, as I went into my second year. My Infant 2 teacher was a lovely, young, kind teacher called Mrs Lenayne – no idea if that was how it should be spelt. She wore Dr Scholl wooden sandals and didn't mind if you tickled her feet when you sat for story time. And even better than that, I learned to read in spite of the Initial Training Alphabet (ITA) a form of phonics that was introduced in the early sixties as an experiment. I was hopeless at it but you weren't allowed to go onto regular reading books until you finished ITA. I vividly remember struggling with the last page of the last book, sitting in the story corner. Eventually I got it and was allowed to progress onto Janet and John books. I don't know if ITA helped or hindered but I do know that once I started regular reading, I had found a passion that I still have today.

In Infant 2 I sat beside a boy called Peter Schofield; we were both quiet. The lovely Mrs Lenayne decided to get two goldfish for the class to look after. Following many suggestions and a class vote the goldfish were duly named Chips and Dreamer! Each week a different pair of children were chosen to go out to the sink in the corridor and change the fish water, a huge honour and one highly sought after. When it came to mine and Peter's turn, we took the globe shaped bowl out, arrived at the sink, looked at each other and realised that neither of us had any idea how on earth you got two fish out of a bowl, cleaned the bowl and got the fish back in. Needless to say, it was traumatic for us and not least the poor fish. Our total ineptitude led to a broken fishbowl and a single fish down the plug hole. I don't recall Mrs Lenayne being angry with us but

I do remember the shame of having to go back into class to tell them all that Dreamers had had his chips!

Another interesting part of my early years was the Whit Walks. I had no understanding of the political and religious significance of them as a child. All I knew was we got new clothes (an unusual event) and we "walked round." I'm not sure if this consisted of only the Catholic schools or not but we paraded through the main streets of the town. Each school had a different uniform and usually a banner with a picture of a saint or martyr that was relevant to their school. The "walking round" was ok but the best part was going round to the neighbours afterwards to show off your new clothes. Everyone gave you money and you came back with a pocket full of sixpences and threepenny bits. I was never allowed to spend any of it, it went straight into my money box, to save for who knows what. I suspect it went into general housekeeping to keep us afloat.

My third and final year at St. Pat's was where I blame my lifelong dislike and hopelessness around maths. The lovely Mrs Lenayne stayed in Infant 2, and Infant 3 brought a young, loud, Irish woman, who had favourites. Sadly, I was not one of them, in spite of having an Irish father and surname!

Half way through the year I got measles which resulted in time off school. When I returned, the class had been doing division sums. I didn't know how to do it. I sat and did a whole page of sums...they were all wrong. I didn't know that until I took them up to be marked. Big red crosses all over the page, not a single one right. I was sent back to my desk to "correct" them. I changed every one of them, proudly took them back up, sure this time they were all right. How could they be, no one had taught me division? Even worse I was sent back in tears because not only were they all wrong but I hadn't rewritten them out, just replaced the old numbers with new ones. I didn't like Infant 3 much although I had friends and loved playing out in the playground.

Somewhere around this time I developed a fear of going to bed. Now it would probably be recognised as an attachment disorder. I don't know how it started but I do remember having an absolute fear of being on my own once the bedroom door was shut. I would start off by calling down every few minutes, "Goodnight, Grandma!" She answered at first but as it went on and on, she stopped, presumably hoping I would too. This resulted in me getting out of bed and going to the top of the stairs just in case she hadn't heard. This always ended in a telling off for being out of bed. Reassured that she was still actually there, the whole process started again. As an adult I can only imagine how exhausting this would have been, particularly for a woman who was now close to her eighties and having to care for a feisty 6-year-old. One night it got so bad that in desperation she tied the dressing gown cord to the banister so I couldn't get out onto the stairs. Undeterred I banged on the window so hard I cracked the pane and a neighbour came over to tell Gran what I'd done.

A couple of days later I was summoned into Sister Camillus's office at school. She never raised her voice but explained that she had heard I was being extremely "naughty" at night. I was utterly mortified. She told me very calmly that I needed to stop all this nonsense and that I had to go to bed and go to sleep without making a fuss. She also said she would send for me in a few days' time to check that I had done what she had said. She never needed to. After that I went to bed and went to sleep. I also got to have the single room to myself so I wouldn't be disturbed when my sister Liz, nine years older than me, went to bed. She was livid because it meant she had to sleep in the big double bed with Gran, and Gran farted...a lot!

The big event in Infant 3 was making our First Confession and First Holy Communion. I think a lot of the prep for it went completely over my head. We had to learn the prayer for the beginning of confession, go into the confessional box, say it along with our list of "sins," take the penance and promise not to do it again. Because I didn't really know what constituted the sins that were not too bad, I had to wing it a bit. I knew murdering someone was a mortal sin and one there was no coming back from but I wasn't sure of the sliding scale of minor sins. I settled on three that I trotted out at every confession I made until I stopped going when I was around eighteen.

The confessional box was a bit like an upmarket Tardis but with no depth. There was a wooden window with a red velvet curtain between you and the priest. It was dark and a bit scary. A quick prompt from Father…I forget his name, and I was off.

"Bless me Father for I have sinned. This is my first confession. I have told lies, (not really, well maybe) and I called someone a bad name and I swore (definitely not)."

This earned me two Hail Mary's and an Our Father which wasn't bad as that absolved me from all the sins I might ever have committed in my 7 years on the planet. I was out with a blessing and a clean soul to take First Holy Communion on Sunday.

The day dawned and I wore a little white dress and a veil. The dress was well above my knee and quite inappropriate really but it was all there was. We had had it drilled into us that under NO circumstances were we to touch the wafer thin "host" because that was the "Body of Christ." We had to sit through Mass which was long and boring, waiting until nearly the end for communion. I'm sure it's the only reason communion comes last because you haven't officially heard Mass if you haven't been there for communion, even if you don't take it. We waited in line nervously, all of us praying Father would put the host far enough on our tongues so that Jesus didn't fall out. When it was your turn the priest held the white wafer circle in front of your face, said, "Body of Christ," and you had to say, "Amen," quickly and then stick out your tongue to receive it. I managed without mishap but no one had told me Jesus would be stuck on the roof of my mouth for ages after and I wondered if scraping him off with your tongue constituted a sin. Fortunately, the communion breakfast in school soon solved that and Jesus was happily munched, along with the egg and cress sandwiches and orange juice!

I moved "home" after Infant 3 and to another school for Junior 1 to Junior 4.

3

The Holy Rosary Years

So, two and a bit years completed at St. Pat's and I was on the move. Gran's house on Eldon Street was actually her son's, my uncle Eric's house. He had bought it as an investment and let his parents live in it when he got married and moved to a "posh" bungalow. The end of my time in Infant 3 coincided with a buy-out of all the houses on the three streets to make way for the new by-pass being built. As most of the households were council tenants they were split between various council estates.

Gran was placed in a retirement bungalow on the estate we lived on, Fitton Hill. The bungalow was quite small and only for retired people so I spent the week at "home" and weekends with her. This proved to be a good arrangement as Gran was literally five minutes away so I went to her house before and after school.

Holy Rosary School

It was too far to go to St. Pat's from our house so I moved to a smaller primary school called Holy Rosary. It was much more modern than St. Pat's but it also had a nun as a Head Mistress – Sister Benignus, Latin for kind...she wasn't always.

There were no transition days or pre visits. I don't even know how I got there but I do remember being joined by another girl, Jennifer, as we got into the classroom. Our Junior 1 teacher was another nun, Sister Collette. She was nice and also quite young; until then I had only met old nuns! She told us to go and choose our desk and I chose the front desk until I was yanked firmly by Jennifer who was far more worldly wise than I and pulled me to the back row. This started a long friendship that I still have with Jennifer to this day. Now it's not more than an odd exchange on Facebook but then we became instant BFA's (Best Friends Always). Jennifer had also been at St. Pat's but in the other class from me so I didn't know her then. I liked Holy Rosary from the start. Sister Collette was a kind, gentle soul, not so Sister Benignus who had a furious temper and once pulled my hair by my pony tail because I turned around in my seat. She wasn't always bad, but she was very scary, especially in assembly when she would point at the words to the hymns with a big stick. The words were up on an enormous scroll, no PowerPoints in those days!

The school, situated beside the church was very invested in the Virgin Mary and a lot of the hymns were dedicated to her. We also "crowned" her on May Sunday, when one of the girls was chosen as the May Queen and processed into church. The poor girl who was chosen had to climb the short ladder in front of a crowded church of proud parents and fidgety children, wait for the hymn to get to the bit that said "Oh Mary we CROWN you" and then place the crown of roses on the head of the statue of Mary. In our year it was a girl called Monica Barrett who was the May Queen and her dad was the deputy head of the senior school I went to later. The rest of us were all dressed in our "walking round" clothes and couldn't wait for it to be over to see the neighbours and get our money. I'm sure Monica couldn't wait for it to be over either.

Holy Rosary Church

Life at Holy Rosary was significantly better than St. Pat's and the transition to living at "home" was ok too. Both Mags and Liz were there, although Mags only until I was eight years old, when she got married, and Liz till I was twelve, when she got married too.

Fitton Hill Library

Our house at 139 Fir Tree Ave was really close to the library and I was there at least two or three times a week. I was like Roald Dahl's Matilda carrying bags of books backwards and forwards all the time.

I rarely watched TV at home, only at Gran's house – she had acquired a TV when she moved. It was from Radio Rentals and she paid a weekly or monthly payment to rent it. It was black and  white because only really posh people had colour TV's but at least it didn't go off mid programme when the two shillings ran out like at home! The two shillings changed to ten pence after decimalisation in 1971 and I remember being at school in Junior Two playing decimal Bingo over the radio. The "oldies" were horrified and convinced it was a conspiracy to devalue their money. I remember Gran saying that now a shilling was only worth five pennies and not twelve, we were being cheated.

I learned to play the violin at Holy Rosary. I didn't want to, I wanted to play the flute or trumpet but I wasn't allowed. Sister Benignus (SB) came into our class one day and said some people were going to play musical instruments. The "chosen" names were duly called out and allocated an instrument. There seemed little logic and definitely no choice in what we were given. I had to play the violin because "your sister, Elizabeth, played it!" I have a lot to thank Liz for, but playing the violin isn't one of them. There were about six of us chosen to play violin but I only remember Pauline Clegg because we once played a duet together at a school concert. Our first teacher was a lovely man called Mr Rushton. If we played well, we got a humbug and he never shouted at us. Then he left…and SB took over the violins. I was absolutely petrified because I had a terrible secret. I couldn't read music! I had no understanding of how Every Good Boy Deserves Favours and FACE translated into being able to read the notes on the page, but being a good girl, I learned the phrases and bluffed it. Most of the time it worked. I went home and practised and practised the pieces until I was note perfect because there was no way I could read the music. I did get caught out massively though when she asked me to play from the fourth bar and stop at the seventh. I just guessed and while regularly getting a good telling off for it I don't think she ever knew I couldn't read music. I gave up the violin the day SB retired which was also my last day of Primary School.

It wasn't only music that was an arbitrary occupation at both Junior and Senior school, sport was too. In much the same way as I was chosen to play violin, Jennifer was chosen to play badminton. No trials, no show of interest, just selected at random. I would have loved to have played and I was pretty good at tennis because Liz used to take me for a knock about at her tennis club. Not that that necessarily translates to being good at badminton. Anyway, that link was too tenuous and even when Jennifer tried to fight my corner, Mr Littleford, a real nice guy who later became Head, told her she couldn't just ask so she could play with her friend!

Neither the violin nor badminton came between us though, and we were firm friends until early secondary school when we did grow apart a bit.

With Gran at my Confirmation

The other "big" event that happened while I was at Holy Rosary was being "confirmed". It wasn't on the same scale as First Holy Communion although I did have a white dress, a long one this time that Liz made for me. I remember very little of it except in the run up to it Sister Benignus told me they couldn't find my records of baptism and I couldn't be confirmed unless I was baptised. I was hauled out of class, taken into church and baptised by Father Dorrington who had replaced old Father Buckley. I don't know whether Dad knew or agreed or not beforehand. He wouldn't have disagreed but whether he was asked remains a mystery, I can only imagine what would happen now if someone was taken out of class and baptised without permission! Dad didn't seem to know about it until I got home and told him. The best thing about confirmation was you got to choose a saint's name to add to your name. Dad thought Wilhemina was a good choice...I didn't! The whole quick baptism thing worked in my favour though, because I told him I had to say my name before they did it and I had chosen Catherine. I honestly think it was one of the only times I lied to him...and I still think it was worth it! So, my full name is Christine Teresa Catherine, although technically the Catherine isn't official and isn't documented anywhere other than parish records as far as I know. Sadly, Holy Rosary Church closed in 2017 so I have no idea if records are still available.

One other thing I remember about my time at Holy Rosary was that we had bomb scares. It was when the "Troubles" in Northern Ireland were at their height and of course we were a Catholic school. As children we were never afraid and had no real understanding of what it was about. My dad was from Belfast and refused to speak about the "Troubles" at home. I knew he had a fear of going "home" and he only went back once, after I was born, for his mother's funeral. Before that the whole family went every summer. The bomb scares at school meant we were evacuated to the playground. As children we had no concept of the seriousness of this and just looked on it as extra playtime. I don't think it happened much at senior school or if it did, I don't remember it being a regular thing, even though the Northern Ireland situation was very prominent at that time.

By the time I went to senior school the eleven plus exam, which enabled kids who passed to go to grammar school, had been abolished. Comprehensive education was the big thing. Two of my older siblings, Eric and Liz had passed and went to Cardinal Langley and Notre Dame senior schools. Eric was taught by the De La Salle Brothers and I think he gave them a good run for their money. He was a bit of a handful especially after Mum died apparently, but as the school was two bus rides away and we didn't have a phone, he got away with a lot of stuff. Liz gave the staff at Notre Dame, who were mostly nuns, but not all, an easier time.

I went to the comprehensive that my older brother John and sister Mags went to. They had left school several years previously as they are sixteen and eleven years older than me. Holy Rosary was a big improvement on my early years at St. Pat's and although we were all a bit nervous about going up to senior school it was just looked upon as the next step. There were no transition days, no preparation and no information, only the expectation that we would turn up and all would be revealed. We did and it was!

4

The St. Anselm's Years

As I said, senior school was just the next thing. It was about a mile and a half from our house. I had no idea where it was or how I was going to get there apart from with Jennifer, my friend I mentioned earlier. I called for her on the first day. Her older brother John had agreed, under pressure, to let us follow him. Under no circumstances were we to speak to him and heaven forbid, say we knew him!

We followed him, all the way into the playground where we met some of our former classmates. We were all a bit nervous and there were other pupils there from other feeder Catholic primary schools. We all wore the same navy-blue uniform, long trousers for boys and skirts for girls (no trousers for girls then!), blue shirts until third year then white. Ties were the same except they had a different coloured stripe for whichever feeder primary school you came from. Holy Rosary was blue. Dad showed me how to tie it but it took me a while to get the hang of it and I hated PE because I could never be sure I'd get it back on and not wearing a tie was a "strapping" offence. It was always called the strap not the belt.

At some point we were ushered into the main hall and names called out as to which class we were going into. There were six classes: A and Alpha were the top classes, B and Beta middle and C and Gamma bottom. I thought there had been a mistake when I was called out for One Alpha. I had a severe case of imposter syndrome and was sure I'd be found out by break time and sent to what I thought sounded like the worst class ever, One Gamma. I wasn't, and I was delighted that there were quite a few of my old classmates in my new form class. Jennifer was one and since her surname was Gill and mine Fitzsimons we were in the same row of desks. My friend Mary Flanagan was also there in the next desk as we sat in alphabetical columns and rows of boy/girl. Sister Mary Pascal, another nun, was our form teacher. Firm but fair, although like many of the teachers not averse to using the strap. She was also our Latin teacher and Jennifer hated it. I loved it though, and didn't mind at all if she copied my homework.

I had a good circle of friends at St. Anselm's, mostly new ones that I made from other feeder schools. Although I did stay friends with Jennifer we slowly drifted apart and chose different subjects. Both Jennifer and Mary left school at sixteen and we lost touch for a few years, only really reconnecting much later through the power of Facebook with Jennifer and more traditional methods with Mary. Now I occasionally "speak" with Jennifer on Facebook which is one of its good points. Mary lives in Ireland and doesn't do social media much so we do send the odd letter but mostly texts at birthdays and Christmas time.

When it came to choosing subjects for O Levels and subsequently A Levels, it was a straight choice between Arts and Sciences. Years later, when my own children were choosing subjects, they had to choose from both disciplines to make sure they had opportunities to follow any career path. Although I know that's the best way, leaving all options open, I was so glad not to have to do sciences. I did have to do maths though which I still hated from Primary School, compounded by an even worse teacher, who will remain nameless, and experience in first year at St. Anselm's. She would teach the lesson on the black board at the front and then to check understanding would come down the rows and you had to work out a sum from the textbook. I was quite close to the front being an F surname so technically my question would have been easier than the later questions but it made no difference. Inevitably I got it wrong. Then there was the agony of waiting for when she would give you a "second chance." Obviously, because it was random, there was no way it could be worked out beforehand. I always got it wrong and then I had to stand on my chair until the lesson was finished. I'm not sure how she thought these methods were going to help someone with a fear of maths, and they didn't.

Thankfully, I had a lovely maths teacher for the next two years but the damage was done. By the time I was in my exam year I did so badly in my mock exam they didn't even put me in for the O Level...great result as far as I was concerned! I did ok in both English Language and Literature as well as Latin, History, RE (good Catholic upbringing) and...Pottery! The latter only because I was so bad at Art, they let me do a branch of it that was just Pottery. The only trouble was it had to be a Certificate of Secondary Education (CSE) qualification which was considered inferior to O Levels, unless you got a Grade One, which grudgingly counted as an O Level. I got a Grade One in Pottery in spite of having no real talent!

PE was another subject that seemed to bring out the worst in those teaching it. Almost all the PE teachers were "strap happy" and only liked to teach the real sporty kids. If you were sporty, you were on every team and definitely got preferential treatment. The rest of us just stood on the sidelines waiting for the lesson to be over and finding ways to avoid the communal showers and the cross-country runs.

I only got the strap twice at senior school, once for hiding in the cloakroom at breaktime because I didn't want to go outside in the cold. That was from the girl's Head Teacher, Mrs Healy. Her strap was long and thin with two leather thongs that whipped up onto the underside of your arm, the sensitive bit. You had to stand with arms out one hand on top of the other, palms up and not move. You got three lashes and had to switch hands in between. If you moved, and they missed, you got an extra one! I think the second time was from Sister Pascal for not doing homework, which really wasn't like me. I had the strap once at primary school too for...fighting! That was definitely NOT like me. I was a real wimp at school and never got into trouble but I was sticking up for a girl I didn't even know that well. The class bully then turned on me and we ended up "scrapping". That was in junior three and I had to sit on my own, on the bus to our weekly swimming lesson, there and back, to think about my behaviour. I was absolutely mortified. I didn't tell anyone at home about getting the "strap". I'm sure Dad would have said I must have deserved it if a teacher said so. Oh, how times have changed and not all for the better.

As I say I had a good crowd of friends at senior school and Bernie Costello was one of the best in the middle years. We fell out grandly though in 5th year because she snogged the school rugby captain who I had an enormous crush on! We did manage to patch things up eventually and I went on to be her chief bridesmaid when she married at twenty-one...not to the rugby captain. That seems so young. Jennifer was another early bride but we weren't really in touch by then. There were also two Angelas. One in my year, who came on holiday with me to Switzerland (another story) and my still good friend Angela Tunnacliffe (Tun) who I met walking to school. She was the year below me so she was never in any of my classes although in sixth form we were together in the Sixth Form Centre. In spite of her living in the USA and me in Scotland for almost forty years, we still manage to meet up most years.

The St. Anselm's years were mostly fun. I discovered "boys" although they didn't really discover me. I did get my first kiss on the Tunnel of Love ride at Blackpool Pleasure Beach on a 5th year school trip though! I loved 5th and 6th years but didn't do a great deal of studying and left with two very unconvincing A Levels in English and RE. They were enough though for me to move onto the next phase in my life.

5

High Days and Holidays

I missed out on family holidays because by the time I came along Mum was already quite poorly and died when I was fourteen months old. Before I was born the rest of the family spent most summer holidays prior to her death in Ireland with our Irish family. Dad would go over with them on the ferry and spend two weeks before coming back for work. Mum and my four siblings stayed on for the duration of the school holidays and sometimes beyond. This meant they occasionally started school in Strangford before coming back to Oldham. They stayed with our Irish grandparents Nanna and Granda who I have no memory of at all. Mags and Liz have always said Nanna was very scary and they tried to stay out of her way but Granda was a gentle soul. There was no shortage of friends for them all in Strangford as my dad's brother and his wife, Uncle John and Auntie Betty, and his sister and her husband, Aunt Norah and Uncle Tommy, had eleven children between them.

I think John and Eric, my older brothers, spent a lot of time "dating" the local girls and were probably off doing their own thing for a large amount of the time!

My holidays were completely different. In my early years I was taken to my great aunt and uncle's house not far from Blackpool. Uncle Harry was my gran's youngest brother and had lived in India with his wife Doreen. I never knew what exactly he did in India other than being "in business." They had three children: two boys, Alan and David, who were around the same ages as my brothers John and Eric, and then a younger daughter, Jane who was severely handicapped and died in late childhood. Their house in Poulton Le Fylde seemed enormous. Lots of bedrooms all with a designated colour and when we arrived, we were told which room we were to sleep in. It always sounded very grand to say, "I'm sleeping in the blue room or the green room!" They also had a "playroom" and a big lounge and an even bigger kitchen. The playroom had lots of books in it which I loved and since their children were too old to play, I had it all to myself. The house was full of paintings and souvenirs from their life in India. They also had a huge back garden where they grew flowers and vegetables in as well as an "orchard." Often, I was sent out to pick peas, beans or lettuce and tomatoes for the evening meal and sometimes I was allowed to eat the grapes out of the greenhouse. They owned a newsagent shop in Fleetwood too which meant they were away most of the day. Gran and I would go into Fleetwood to the beach and then meet them back at the shop to get a lift home.

Donkey Rides

Sometimes I had a donkey ride at the beach and sometimes an ice cream, but never both. Uncle Harry was quite gruff and I was scared of him. He once gave me a huge row because I had my elbows on the table with my fork in the air and it jagged his arm as he reached over for the peas. They went all over the table and I was left mortified, mostly because we were brought up to have impeccable table manners and I knew it was rude to have elbows on the table. Auntie Doreen and Uncle Harry were used to having "servants" in India and had obviously lived a lavish lifestyle. They were very kind but we always felt like the poor relations and that we never really came up to spec.

Auntie Doreen also knitted a lot, not just for me but for my dolls and teddies too. She was very talented and was able to rustle up a little outfit for "Honey Bear" my childhood teddy (which I still have) or Janet my beloved dolly (which I don't have). She seemed to do this with apparent ease while watching Coronation St!

I went back to Uncle Harry and Auntie Doreen's with Liz when she was in her teens and I was seven or eight. We went into Blackpool on the bus which wasn't far and she took me to the Waxworks Museum and the Tower. I think Gran stayed at home for a rest! I went again with Mags a couple of times when Simon, her son, was a baby. Again, we did the beaches at both Blackpool and Fleetwood as well as spending time in Stanley Park. For the most part, our holidays were good fun and we felt lucky to be able to go. I also went to Uncle Harry and Auntie Doreen's with John and his wife and their eldest son Matthew who was a baby at the time.

Uncle Harry, Matthew, Me and Auntie Doreen

Our next-door neighbours were lovely people and I was very fond of them both. Alice was like a mother to me and in my early years Granville was the only person I knew who had a car. He worked for Eagle Star Insurance and had a Hillman Imp that he took me and Alice out in on Sundays. Sometimes we went to New Brighton, just outside Liverpool. It's probably only about half an hour in the car but then it felt like it was hundreds of miles away. We had some memorable times and I know they looked on me as the daughter they never had in spite of being very happy with their two sons, Brian and Bernard.

I also used to go to another of Gran's siblings for holidays too. Auntie Mary lived in a tiny village called Sheet in Petersfield, Hampshire. She had lived with her other sister, Margaret, who died when I was about four. I think she had been a Matron of a hospital. Mary had been a Head Teacher of a Primary School before she retired. She was ahead of her time and had spent a year in Australia on a Head Teacher Programme before retiring. She was a wonderful lady who was firm and stood no nonsense but kind and always took time to explain things. I don't ever remember her teaching me anything academic but she was very into gardening and grew her own fruit and vegetables. She would take me on walks and point out flowers and trees and birds. She seemed to know so much about so many things. I loved her house. It was a bungalow with a dormer window and I had never seen a bungalow before until Grandma moved into one. I stayed with Auntie Mary a few times as a child with Grandma, but also as a young adult on my own.

Auntie Mary had a big garden that circled the house on all sides. The bungalow was set back from the road in a tiny hamlet of three or four houses. It was right in the middle of the countryside and was the most peaceful, beautiful place, teeming with wildlife. I was always happy to just hang around the house and garden when I went to stay with her. Even now it's my "happy place" when I do a visualisation meditation or have to think of a favourite time and place. There was also a village fair every year and several times I was there for that. She entered me into the cake baking competition and taught me to bake a Victoria sponge. It was a valiant effort but I didn't win. She also tried to teach me how to make a miniature flower arrangement in a bottle top...I definitely didn't win that!

In Junior three I went on a school trip to the Isle of Man. I couldn't believe I was allowed to go but the school let us pay up the price of the holiday every week for almost a year. It was £17 and that included full board as well as 50p per day spending money! It was the most fantastic holiday. We caught the ferry from Liverpool and what a rough crossing it was! Even the teachers suffered from seasickness. Everyone soon forgot about it though as we had a brilliant week. They took us to the Laxey Wheel and Summerland which was an indoor activity park that burned down a couple of years later. We walked for miles around the island taking in the sights. We even had a cinema trip to see Bedknobs and Broomsticks. All that fun for £17!

We had been told that on the final night there was to be a fancy dress competition and my brother Eric was determined I was going to win. He set about making my costume himself. It was the early seventies and Britain was almost on its knees with strikes. Oldham was very working class and we had our share of hardships due to the strikes. Eric bought boxes of matches and then stuck the boxes as well as the individual matchsticks all over an old dress of mine. Then he made a placard to hang around my neck saying "No More Strikes!" I won first prize, I'm not even sure what the prize was, nothing significant I don't think; but I was delighted even though the costume had taken up a lot of room in my suitcase. I'm pretty sure the matches weren't struck and I can only imagine that now, with all the health and safety rules around, I would definitely not have been allowed to dress in it!

Fancy dress night – Isle of Man Back row fourth from right

Another couple of holidays I had were with Mags when she took me to Mablethorpe in a caravan and later to Spain. We went with her first husband and my nephew Simon who was just a baby. I was around ten. Mablethorpe was a real bucket and spade holiday and I was still young enough to enjoy donkey rides on the beach.

Then we flew with Dan Air to Lloret de Mar on the Costa Brava when I was an early teen. It was my first package holiday and it felt very "swanky" to be eating in a hotel every night being served by waiters and waitresses. It was a whole new world and one I didn't repeat until after I started work and was able to pay for myself.

Simon, Mags and Me at Mablethorpe

Eric had joined the army when I was around three years old but he was really good at sending letters to me and Grandma and he always sent presents, usually a doll dressed in national costume, from wherever he was based. I had a lovely collection from

Cyprus, Singapore and Hong Kong. When he came home on leave, he always took me out for a treat, one time to Belle Vue Zoo in Manchester, which closed several years later. I remember him picking me up and running fast to get round to an enclosure because a peacock had opened its tail! He also took me on day trips to Blackpool and Southport but I was always so travel sick it must have been a nightmare for him.

Eric loved the Beatles. I'm not sure if he was "babysitting" me one day or if he just decided to treat me to a trip to the cinema. Anyway, we went to see "A Hard Day's Night" which he was desperate to see. Unfortunately, it was during a phase when I was afraid of the dark. The minute the lights went down I screamed and cried until he had to take me out! Eventually Eric bought himself out of the army so that he could pursue a semi-professional football career. He was quite successful but when that came to an end he played rugby league, again semi-professional, as both a player and coach. He was quite a celebrity in our home town and was very popular with the girls! He went into teaching, Physical Education (PE) and quickly became head of department at Breeze Hill School. He was a very good big brother and amongst other things arranged for me to have swimming lessons through a swimming club that one of his colleagues ran. Dad couldn't have afforded lessons at the local pool but he paid for my bus fares, two buses each way, twice a week. I swam for two or three years and became quite a strong swimmer. It was while Eric was at Breeze Hill and then afterwards at Failsworth School, that he somehow managed to wangle me on two school trips. One to Lausanne in Switzerland and one to France, I don't even remember whereabouts in France. The first trip to Lausanne I didn't know anyone but soon made friends and had a great time. The trip to France though was obviously undersubscribed and I was allowed to take a friend with me. I took Angela Clarke, one of my best friends at the time. We had a blast. It was during a very brief punk rock phase for me and I bonded with a French boy, Gilbert, over a rendition of Ca Plane Pour Moi by Plastic Bertrand! We became pen pals for a few months after but it soon fizzled out!

Day trips from school weren't regular events but I think in 3rd or 4th year we had a day trip to Blackpool. It always seemed so far away and yet it's only about an hour from Oldham. Anyway, this was the place I had my first real kiss! I'd fancied a boy in my class for months and we were part of a big group that hung around together. He was in the school brass band which was very cool back in the day and he also played in a pop/rock band with his elder brother who later taught with my brother Eric. Anyway, we started out with the group and even held hands for a bit before deciding to go on the Tunnel of Love boat ride. Most of it was in the dark and at some point, we had our first kiss. It was nice but nothing more than that and we never really got together afterwards although we continued to hang around with the same crowd until we left sixth form.

My sister Liz was engaged but then met her new boyfriend Craig, (her future husband) who had a very cool car. An RS200 at first, and then the ultimate as far as me and my friends were concerned, a Ford Capri. I used to watch from the window as he came to pick Liz up. He didn't often come into the house he just parked outside. Once, he and Liz picked me up at school, for lunch, in a Jaguar! It was a company car but my "cool" ratings went up several notches. Craig was a Speedway fan and Liz and I became fans too. Most weekends they took me to the race track at Belle Vue to see the Belle Vue Aces as the team were called. We went to most home meets and even down to Wembley once and also Kings Lynn, both trips there and back in a day.

Belle Vue Zoo in Manchester was a rare treat and I remember going there with Eric once and also with my gran's brother, Uncle Willie, which was when I got to hold a monkey and feed it! I always wanted to ride on the back of the elephants which paraded up and down the zoo but I think it was too expensive and now it would definitely be politically incorrect!

6

Hobbies and Interests

When I consider the hobbies and activities that are available to children nowadays it's mind boggling. I remember even when Paul and Suzy were younger we were a constant taxi service to gymnastics, football, swimming, tennis, dancing, rugby and they were just the regular ones that they stuck at.

As a child a hobby that cost money was a luxury and was a definite one thing only, if at all. Most of our time, as previously mentioned, we "played out." We didn't need to be taken to tennis or football or anywhere else because these were games we played on the street, rotating with the seasons and what props and equipment we had available.

I have vague memories when I lived on Eldon Street, of Gran taking me to ballet lessons. It didn't last. I seem to remember standing in a line of wannabe ballerinas and having no clue what the teacher wanted me to do and absolutely no interest in doing it!

The Coronettes – the dance troupe I wasn't allowed to join!

When I moved to Fir Tree Ave, the library was just a couple of minutes away and I found reading. I loved it, I read voraciously and was a constant visitor to Fitton Hill Library. Sometime after I met Jennifer, she started to go to the youth club on Wednesday night to "Troupe Dancing." I think it's very much a north of England thing as I've never come across it anywhere else. It was a mix of formations, thigh slapping, acrobatics and gymnastics. It was extremely popular and I was desperate to do it. It was however one of the few things that Dad and Gran agreed on. Gran saw no sense in "parading about half dressed" and Dad thought there was no need to "slap your thighs until they turned red!" I was devastated. The troupe was called the Coronets and they had short, sparkly costumes not unlike cheerleaders of today. They trained on Wednesday evenings and then on Saturdays during the summer competed at local carnivals. The ultimate being Oldham Carnival. This was the highlight of the summer in our hometown. There was a big parade that processed through the town and down into Alexandra Park, ending on the big playing field. The playing field was transformed into a funfair and competition site. The Coronets were at the top of their game, always with the best and highest human display. Jenn was like a rubber doll bending and twisting and being thrown in the air. I could only watch enviously. In truth, being a bit chubby at this stage it was probably a blessing that no one had to throw me in the air and catch me!

As a consolation, I don't know who decided or how, I was allowed to go to First Aid at the youth club on Wednesdays! It was run by an older couple, The Fentons, who were members of the St. John's Ambulance Brigade. It wasn't troupe dancing but it was something and so off I went every Wednesday evening to learn First Aid and Home Nursing. Exciting it wasn't and I found every excuse to have to go out to the bathroom so I could sneakily watch the Coronets in the big hall! I did it for a few years but never got to use my bandaging and splinting skills until I was nursing years later.

Another hobby that was too expensive was swimming lessons. Again, I was desperate to go because Jennifer went. Her mum took me a couple of times but the swim teachers were grumpy women in severe looking swimsuits and flowery swim hats. They were totally unimpressed by my heroic efforts to swim with one foot safely on the bottom of the pool!

Eric came to the rescue with this one though as I've mentioned elsewhere, and as Head of PE, managed to get me into a swim club that I went to twice a week. His colleague was a good teacher and I attribute my ability to swim decently to her.

Apart from these things I had very few hobbies. There just wasn't money or availability. I played on the netball team at Holy Rosary and I was an "Oxo girl" on Saturday morning for the boys' football team. That meant making Oxo for the two teams at half time and cutting up the oranges into wedges for them to suck on…what a combination!

At St. Anselm's I was a member of the senior girls' choir. It was pretty much an in-school activity during lunchtimes but we did do a couple of concerts at various times in the evenings. We also got to sing sometimes with the brass band which was always a bonus because there were a lot of males in the brass band. Indeed, my big crush and first kiss on the Tunnel of Love in Blackpool was a member of the brass band!

As student nurses, my friend Penny and I would have phases of "fitness" and we occasionally jogged but the phases never lasted long as we were often on opposite shifts and our social lives were too good for exercise! When I moved to Edinburgh I joined a local fitness centre, next to the Corstorphine Inn, and did aerobics and step classes intermittently.

It's only been since my "middle years" that I have consistently had hobbies that I have stuck at. I started yoga and writing classes in my early fifties and have continued with both. Reading has always been a constant, sometimes more regularly than others but I can't imagine not having a book on the go. I'm not sure if mindfulness counts as a hobby or is just a way of life but I meditate daily and again can't imagine not doing. My other "woo woo" pursuits are reiki, Indian head massage and crystals. The former two I have trained as a practitioner in although really only use it with family and friends.

Since retiring in 2022 from school I have a mix of "hobbies" and activities that keep me busy. The latest exercise classes being Body Pump which is a weight class and so along with that, yoga and walking and some Spin Cycling I'm hoping to cover all potential pitfalls in my old age. Yoga for flexibility, Body Pump for strength and bone health and walking and cycling for cardio and then there's Wild Swimming which gets a whole section to itself.

Wild Swimming

Swimming is definitely a misnomer. Like many people I took up new hobbies during lockdown. The criteria was often as simple as anything that got you out of the house and stopped you going stir crazy. We walked, we cycled and we "dooked." A lovely Scottish word that sums up perfectly what we do. We dip. I stupidly started this at the most inappropriate time of year in Scotland, February!

I read the books, did my homework, joined the Facebook page and headed down to a local beach, Wardie Bay. Peter came too but only for safety reasons and made it absolutely clear he wasn't participating. Nothing prepared me for the shock of the water temperature, around six degrees centigrade, but I was hooked. I lasted about thirty seconds that day and I have never felt cold like it. I bought a wetsuit but hated it, it was so hard to get on and off. I persevered without the wetsuit and my Maltese friend Cecelia joined me too. For many months it took us longer to get there and undress than we ever spent in the water but it is the most amazing feeling. The sea is cold and can be unpredictable but there is a good community of swimmers and dookers alike at Wardie Bay. It took off massively during lockdown and it's a place you can always find a soul mate who's as daft as you! Much as I liked Wardie Bay though, I'm not the biggest fan of salt water and so a group of us now mostly swim up at the local reservoir, Harlaw Reservoir in Edinburgh. It is the most beautiful, tranquil place with stunning scenery and wildlife and is definitely my "happy place." My neighbours Jane and Ann and friends Mags and Laura are regular "weekend dookers." There's nothing to beat a bracing dook followed by a cup of tea and a "blether" beside one of the most beautiful places in the world. Seriously, everyone should try it...at least once!

7

Toys, Games and Hanging Out

We didn't have a lot of toys growing up, we didn't actually need them because as I said earlier, we "played out" and mostly used stuff that was lying around to play with. A washing line doubled as a skipping rope and we collected elastic bands from the postman and joined them together to make a game that has many names. We called it American skipping but others called it French skipping or elastics. It was a group game and you needed two or three people who held the elastics round various parts of their legs – starting with ankles, to calves, knees and going as high as the waist. Again, there was a whole series of moves and jumps that you had to do correctly before you moved up and if you made a mistake you had to be the one who was keeping the elastics up. There were no rhymes for this game as with skipping. If there were a few people playing we played triangles and it was like a constant flow until someone was "out" and then they took their turn holding the elastics.

We also played marbles at Holy Rosary out in the playground. There was a small earthy patch of compacted earth that we used and we would make a small well with the heel of our shoe. Then you challenged someone to play. This involved suggesting something like "three up" meaning you played for three marbles. A big marble was known as a "Dobber" and was worth ten smaller marbles and the really pretty, unusual marbles were called "Beauts." The game started from a couple of metres (yards in those days) from the hole and you both agreed on the distance. Then taking it in turns you threw your marbles trying to get them in or closest to the hole. As with all our games there were arbitrary rules that were made up and decided on before the game started. Some of the games were tense and I remember two of the boys from my class playing a game of "ten up dobbers" so ten big marbles each. Almost the whole school was there to watch and it was as exciting as any Olympic event I've ever seen! I don't remember us playing marbles at either St. Pat's and certainly not at St. Anselm's – definitely not cool!

When I was very young, I did have a doll's pram, an old-fashioned carriage type which was an ugly green colour but I loved it and my dolls. I had four dolls Janet and Wendy and a black doll called Mandy which was quite a novelty back then. The one I wanted most was a "Tiny Tears" doll though but they were very expensive being one of the most "wanted" toys on every girl's list. You could feed them with water and they would cry real tears and then by the process of gravity the doll would wet its nappy and you had to change it. I so desperately wanted one, especially as a lot of my friends had one. Eventually, and I'm not sure who bought it, I got the smaller version, Teeny Tiny Tears and I loved her! I played with all my dolls until I was quite old by today's standards, around ten years old, I think. I also always wanted a Sindy doll or better still a Tressy doll because Tressy's hair grew out of her head. I never got either but I did get a cheaper version that I called Carol and my great Auntie Doreen made her a whole wardrobe of very "snazzy" clothes. I remember a tangerine-coloured coat with a matching beret and a green pom pom on top!

Honey Bear

The love of my life though was always Honey Bear. Apparently, I got him for my first birthday although no one remembers who from. He is a small "golden" (not anymore!) teddy and I took him with me everywhere. Once when I was about five years old, Liz took me to Alexandra Park and Honey Bear came too, except he didn't come home. I had left him on the swing beside the one I was on. I was distraught and Liz, to her credit, walked all the way back, which wasn't a short distance and luckily, he was still there. Again, great Auntie Doreen knitted for him and they are the clothes he still has to this day. His woollen shorts are a bit tight because I think they ended up in the dryer and went rough but his little red cardigan is still smart! Sadly, he is very much in need of a hip replacement and possibly a little spruce up. I keep threatening to put him on The Repair Shop but so far, I never have...watch this space! He sits on the shelf beside my bed and is still as handsome as ever.

Most of our toys and games we made up ourselves as I said. We did have Snakes and Ladders and Ludo at Grandma's which we played in the evening. Having recently been in a classroom with very young children I think we totally underestimate the value of these simple, cheap games. Taking turns, counting one square at a time, recognising numbers on a dice and realising that you don't always win were all skills that we picked up incidentally. I'm sure there are other skills that children pick up now from electronic games but I think we're missing out on some fantastic learning opportunities for them by not playing simple board games. Cards also featured in our games at home and we learned to recognise numbers, shapes, colours and denominations all subliminally. We added and subtracted and matched and sorted and played "Patience" and "Clock Face" when we were on our own. We played "Fish" and "Pairs" when we were younger and then graduated to "Rummy" and "Trumps" and when Mags was with her first husband his family played "New Market" which was a fast-paced gambling game that they played for pennies or buttons, I often came out of that one with a pile of pennies to spend! Fortunately, the stakes were so low no one turned to gambling as a result of our card games.

I played cards a lot with dad after Liz got married and left home. We didn't have a TV at 118 Fir Tree Ave because neither of us was that interested. Dad listened to the radio and I read a lot but often after dinner we would get the cards out and play for a couple of hours or more. Mostly Rummy but occasionally Trumps. Looking back, I don't think I appreciated the time we spent together but I do now. We never spoke much at all and if we did it was about everyday mundane stuff. He never spoke about my mum to me and I never asked. I often wonder now if I had asked would he have told me about her. It was I guess that he was just a man of his time and not used to opening up and I always felt it would be upsetting for everyone else if I asked about her because they would remember and miss her.

Uncle Eric, Mum's brother could always be relied on for good Christmas and birthday presents. Mostly it was clothes because money was tight and we usually got what we needed, not what we wanted, but occasionally we did get a toy or a game. The best ever was one Christmas when I was about seven or eight, I was always at "home" for Christmas as Grandma went to Uncle Harry and Auntie Doreen's near Blackpool. I was so excited and went off to bed, waking a little after midnight. I was convinced that I had been disturbed by Father Christmas and that was why I was awake. I looked outside and it was snowing heavily. The world was white and there was no one else around. Dad was at midnight mass at Holy Rosary and maybe Liz and Mags were there too or just out! Eric also came in possibly from Mass but unlikely! Anyway, I decided to go downstairs and see if Father Christmas had been…he had! There was a stack of presents, mostly clothes, and an enormous big box. I opened it there and then, not even thinking it wasn't morning and there was no one around. It was "Mouse Trap!" Probably the game of the year and one I hadn't even dreamt of ever getting. It was from Uncle Eric and Auntie Emily.

I had the box open and all the pieces out when Dad came in from church. I was shooed off to bed and couldn't wait until the morning. I loved that game and played it often even though it was a faff to set up and it never ever worked the whole sequence out without a hitch! I was amused recently when I went to help Suzy with her class. They were doing a "history" lesson on toys and she'd managed to get a Mouse Trap game. The kids loved it and so did I. Although the old frustrations surfaced when the ball didn't roll down the stairs properly, all the pieces came undone when we turned the crank and the green man didn't jump backwards into the bucket every time!

Another Christmas at home I asked for a two-wheeler bike. I had a tricycle but I wanted the real thing. Dad wouldn't hear of it and said the roads were too busy...I wonder what he'd make of them now! Whenever friends had a bike, I always asked for a turn on them and I had taught myself to ride a two-wheeler without stabilisers. I was excited to wake up on Christmas morning but sadly no bike. Dad was adamant, but I did get a two-wheeler blue scooter that I absolutely loved. Incredibly, the local paper shop at "The Green" was open and I set off with Liz to scoot to the shop. No idea what we went to buy on Christmas day and why it was even open, but it was. I seem to remember getting sweets of some kind and I scooted back happily. It was only when I got home that dad asked if I'd found the sixpence piece on the plate. I hadn't, but when I looked it was still there! Although I never got a bike, I didn't hold a grudge and it would have made no difference anyway if I did! No, meant no!

When I met Peter, I must have told him I had always wanted a bike and lo and behold on my birthday I got a shiny new one, I loved it and it was worth waiting till my 25th birthday to get it!

Although I was an avid reader, we had almost no books in the house. As I previously mentioned the library was a home from home for me and I borrowed books at a phenomenal rate.

One thing we were never allowed to be was bored. If we ever said it, we would immediately be found a "job" to do which could be anything from dusting to peeling potatoes or vegetables. There was no expectation, even if we were bored, that an adult would jump in and amuse us either and there was no money around to join clubs or activities on a regular basis. As a young child I would play for hours at "hospitals," "schools" or set up "camp" under the table. The camp also served as a ship, a den, or wherever else my imagination took me. My trusted dolls and teddies were my patients, pupils and fellow adventurers until I was fed up enough to head outside to see what was going on or call on a friend. Gran liked to walk and could always be relied upon to take me to the park. Alexandra Park was about a half hour walk from Fitton Hill, maybe less. We often walked there after lunch but I have been known to go there myself on many occasions when Gran wasn't available to go. I never told anyone where I was, I just went. Now I look back and think how risky it probably was...or not! I was definitely under ten years old when I did it and on more than one occasion I was "flashed" at. Of course, I didn't tell anyone because I shouldn't have been there in the first place and I would certainly not have been allowed to go back. I don't remember being particularly traumatised by it although I always ran as fast as I could and was fortunately never pursued. Mags also remembers the same but again, would never have dreamt of saying anything.

Once I moved "home" and had met Jennifer we were often round at each other's houses to play. We used the Fitton Hill Primary School playground as our personal playground in spite of it not being our school. It backed onto both Gran's and Jennifer's back garden. Even when Jennifer didn't come out to play, I spent hours hitting a tennis ball against the big school wall, dreaming of being the youngest player at Wimbledon. Sadly, Tracy Austin beat me to it and once the draw of being the youngest player couldn't apply, I lost interest! I did play tennis occasionally with Liz who sometimes took me to the Albion Tennis Club in Ashton and let me hit a few balls over the net. She and Eric also used to play on the courts at Alexandra Park and I would hang out there with them but I never played with them, I was too young.

As I got older "play' was replaced by "hanging out" and by that time I was friends with Mary Flanagan as well as Jennifer. Mary's parents were Irish, from southern Ireland, and always made me welcome. She had an older sister and a younger brother and I spent time at her house a lot in my Holy Rosary years. Jennifer and I had our ups and downs but still hung out together and once even bought a pack of five Park Drive cigarettes and a box of matches and hid behind a lorry to smoke them. I had one puff and that was enough. I've never smoked since. I think Jenn did for a while and I know she used to like the odd cigar but I'm not sure if she still does now.

As I entered my teen years and went to Senior School I had a good circle of friends. We would hang out in Copster Hill Park which was close to school so I guess accessible to us all. Around about the third year our circle widened to include boys and there were a few "pairs" that came out of it but none that lasted. Not me though, I had my sights set on the school rugby captain who was the year above us and didn't know of my existence! It was all very innocent and nothing lasted longer than a couple of weeks of hand holding for anyone. I would have been delighted to have held hands with the rugby captain even for a couple of weeks but sadly it wasn't to be!

As teens we sometimes went to the ice rink in Altrincham which was the other side of Manchester for us and involved two buses and usually cost more money than I had to spend. One time we went and my "beau" from the Tunnel of Love first kiss episode fell and someone sliced over his finger. That involved a certain number of stitches and put paid to his trumpet playing for a few weeks. It didn't deter us though; we just always wore gloves after that!

Things like ice skating were a rare treat and I realised at an early age if I wanted to do stuff, I had to fund it myself and so from thirteen I always had a "Saturday job."

8

Tweens and Teens

Home life evolved as I grew up. The reversal in child care arrangements, when I stayed home during the week and went to Grandma's at the weekend, changed too. When Liz and I moved home Mags was there, Eric was in the army and John had moved out so it was we three girls and Dad. We lived on a relatively new council estate called Fitton Hill which was hailed as flagship estate back in the day. The families that lived there were decent, working-class people. We had a nice four bedroomed house at 139 Fir Tree Ave which we had got before Mum died.

It had two rooms downstairs as well as a kitchen, an outhouse with a coal cellar and a big garden. We also had an indoor toilet downstairs and a bath and toilet upstairs...the lap of luxury! Fir Tree Ave along with Keswick Ave (where Jennifer lived) was the main artery running through the centre. It was tree lined and all the houses had gardens front and back. There was also a wide foot path with grass verges on either side between both the road and the gardens. In more recent years the outer ones have become parking bays.

Mags didn't hang around for long after I moved home! She had a boyfriend and was also training to be a nurse in Ashton, the next town from us. She spent a lot of time there and then got married when I was eight so it was back to Liz and I at home. By this time Liz had a job in the Civil Service in the Valuation Department. She also had a boyfriend, Malc who was a painter and decorator. They got engaged, he completely re-decorated our house and then she met her future husband, Craig, he of the RS200 and Capri!

Malc left me his very trendy (now very retro) record player which was turquoise. I still remember stacking up the EP's (ten I think) and watching in fascination as one finished and the next one dropped down. Technology at its best!

The middle years of my childhood were, as I have already said, slightly unconventional in terms of us not being a typical nuclear family. Often in childhood and early teens all you ever want to do is fit in and not be different. There were situations that I found hard. I hated parent's evenings at both Holy Rosary and St. Anselm's, I don't remember them at all from St. Pat's, there probably weren't any. Dad was a few years older than mum and she was thirty-nine when she had me so he would have been in his mid to late fifties when I was at school. Everyone else's parents seemed young, and they were, people did marry young then. Mum would have been in her early twenties when she had my eldest brother, John.

Dad wasn't always able to come for my parent's nights or concerts because he was working but when he did, I'm ashamed to say I was embarrassed. On several occasions I was asked by the other kids at school why my grandad had come and then I was faced with the double whammy of telling them he was actually my dad and my mum was dead. We didn't really speak about mum at home, it was always a bit of a taboo subject. I think this was only because he found it hard and was of a generation who just carried on. Bereavement counselling wasn't a thing and I believe people thought then it was just too upsetting to keep talking about someone who had died. Grandma didn't speak about mum much either. This obviously rubbed off on me and I never brought up the subject of my mum with either of them in case I upset them.

We weren't unlike many of the families on our estate who struggled with the cost of living. We were lucky though, we always had hot food and although we didn't have central heating at home in either house on Fitton Hill we had plenty of bedding and hot water bottles. We had a coal fire at 139 but it was never lit in the morning because that would have been a waste as we would get up, have breakfast and go out to school or work. No one was home during the day so the fire didn't get lit until evening. Eventually, we had gas fires in both the downstairs rooms and a gas fire at the smaller house, 118 Fir Tree Ave, when Dad and I moved there. We were very aware of the cost of heating and were only allowed one "burner" of the fire, otherwise known as "miser rate!" Both houses were cold and I often went next door to Alice and Granville's to keep warm or round to Grandma's at North Croft, she had central heating once she moved from Eldon Street, which was an unheard-of luxury.

One of the things I hated most about being in a single parent family was free school meals. Everyone knew you weren't paying because you didn't get a dinner ticket like those who paid, you had to get ticked off on a register. I longed to have a dinner ticket but I never got one.

We also got free or subsidised school uniforms which were the most old-fashioned, hideous clothes and made you stick out like a sore thumb. I remember at St. Anselm's when short pencil skirts and round toed shoes were all the rage, all I could get with the CO-OP vouchers was a below knee pleated skirt and winkle picker type shoes. I was mortified and hated it.

I saw as I got older that most of my friends had two parents and almost all of them worked. The women, usually part time. We had a big bakery, Park Cake Bakery, close to where we lived that supplied cakes and bread to not only local shops but bigger retailers like Marks and Spencers. They often took on casual workers during the summer and Christmas and as Saturday workers. I think both Liz and Mags had part time jobs there. It was always a joke at school that if you didn't work hard the only job you'd ever get was putting the cherries on top of the cakes at "Park Cake!"

Two workers in a family certainly made life easier and I saw some of my close friends' families becoming more affluent as we got older. Most, by the time I was in late junior school, had coloured TV's and house phones and some even a family car. We had none of those things, not even when it was just dad and I at home. When we moved to 118 Fir Tree Ave, we didn't even have a TV and neither of us felt its loss. I read avidly and listened to Radio One, Dad also listened to the radio but not Radio One!

Dad didn't read books but always had an evening newspaper. I think my love of books came from Grandma, who was a keen reader until she lost her eyesight. Books were free to borrow from the library and as well as the small local library on Fitton Hill we had the Central Library in the middle of Oldham. I didn't get there very often but it was like an Aladdin's Cave when I did. I loved just being in it and of course there was always so much more choice of books than in our small library. My brothers read less than me and my sisters, but they still read. After John got married, he subscribed to Readers Digest and they did abridged books which were always good for a read when I babysat.

I babysat a lot growing up. As I say, I had nieces and nephews since I was nine years old. I spent a lot of time with Mags when my nephew was a baby, and I often looked after him which was quite usual in spite of my young age. Sometimes on Saturday night I stayed at John's and babysat his two boys, Matthew and Andrew. I was quite adept at changing nappies, feeding babies and generally helping out. Eric's two boys, Daniel and Michael, were usually babysat by his mother-in-law so although I saw them quite a bit, I didn't do much babysitting for them. When Liz had Natalie, I was living with them briefly, and I also turned eighteen. I babysat a lot for Natalie, even overnight when Liz and Craig went away for weekends, but less so Gareth, her younger brother and also Laura, Mags' youngest, because by the time they were born I had already started nursing and wasn't around as often. When I moved to Scotland though Natalie, Gareth and Laura were frequent visitors and in turn babysat my children!

I spent quite a lot of time visiting Liz and her family when they moved just outside Glasgow and Penny and I had some wild times up there! Unfortunately, Liz moved back south before my life in Scotland began so we never lived there at the same time.

Life between Gran's and home continued although in my early and mid-teens I spent more time with my nephews and nieces than at home. Gran also lost most of her sight which was a massive blow to her as she was such a keen reader. She used to get "Talking Books" from the Royal Society for the Blind and the big cassette cartridges were delivered once a fortnight. They also loaned her a huge cassette player to play them on and it did help a lot.

Losing her eyesight and my increasing independence caused a huge decline in her mental health. She suffered terribly with depression and had what would now be considered "breakdowns." Gran was hospitalised several times in my teens and underwent electroconvulsive therapy. I think this was very traumatic although it did seem to help as she came home from hospital until the next bout of depression took over. The ward she was in was right at the bottom of the hospital grounds, tucked away as only psychiatric hospitals and units were. It was known locally as the "Bottom Block" and everyone knew if you went there you, "weren't right in your head." I hadn't appreciated until I was much older that she had also been hospitalised after my mum was born with severe postpartum depression. She certainly had her fair share of mental health problems although her physical health was good.

Just around the time I took my O Levels, Gran had her most severe breakdown, and before she was eventually admitted to hospital, Eric and his wife Bev, and Liz and I took it in turns to stay over with her every night. We stayed in twos, me with Eric and Liz with Bev, I can't remember how long that went on for, a few nights perhaps or a week at the most. Both my brother John and sister Mags had young families at this time so weren't involved.

Eventually, after a failed suicide attempt at home and another lengthy hospitalisation, she was deemed unfit to live on her own and was admitted to a care home two bus rides away. I'm ashamed to say I didn't visit as often as I should have and she died in Greenacres Lodge, a care home, about a year after I started my nurse training. She was in her early nineties and had a brain haemorrhage. My overriding memory of the care home was the smell of stale food and bodily fluids which was extremely unpleasant. I often wonder now how she coped in there without her daily routines and cleaning regime. She would have hated it, I'm sure.

Fir Tree Ave – 139 would have been on the right just out of view

When Liz got married, I was twelve and Dad and I were left rattling about in the four bedroomed house. The rent was expensive and council houses were at a premium even then and so we asked for a transfer. We wanted to stay local as Gran still lived close at this point and was still a big part of my life. We moved to the other side of the road, still Fir Tree Ave, but it was smaller, darker and not nearly as nice a house. It was right outside the bus stop too so everyone "gawped" into my bedroom window when the bus stopped. I didn't really like this house but apart from the bus stop situation I had a decent sized bedroom and as a teenager it's where I spent my time at home.

Dad was working in one of the old cotton mills at the time, Raven Mill, which had been converted into a catalogue warehouse. He was a security guard. It's funny now thinking of buying things from a catalogue although not too different from buying online I suppose. I spent many happy hours thumbing through the sections thinking what I'd buy if we were rich. We weren't and there was very little spending to be done. Dad worked a twelve-hour day shift or night shift. When he was on night shift I stayed

Me and Dad

in the house on my own, I was never scared or thought anything was odd about it. I knew the neighbours were there if I needed anything and Gran around the corner. We got along fine. Dad was a quiet unassuming man who showed very little emotion. I only remember a couple of times him speaking about mum and then it was only a reference to her. He never remarried but according to Jennifer, whose step dad went to the local pub that Dad went to, there was a woman who fancied him! I lived in hope for a while of getting a step-mum but it never happened.

Dad and I had a good system. He shopped and cooked, he had been a cook in the army. I only cooked occasionally or if he was working, and then only for myself. It was my job to go to the launderette and wash and dry the clothes. I loved it because the launderette was right next to the library. I'd put the washing in, head into the library and pop back to swap it into the dryer. I was also supposed to do the housework but in spite of Gran's best teaching I didn't really do a lot. In fairness neither of us made much mess. I did always do the washing up though and we left the dishes to drain, something that was absolutely not allowed at Gran's house!

I stayed on at school into sixth form, only really because I didn't have a clue what I wanted to do. At one point I wanted to join the police and then found out my hereditary bunions excluded me from joining. Not to be deterred I took myself off to the doctor, told him the problem and was listed for surgery. I finished school in June, had the operation (both feet at the same time) in July as I turned eighteen in August. After spending two weeks in hospital I decided I didn't want to join the police after all, I was going to be a nurse!

One thing I was definite about was that I didn't want to stay in my home town and so I applied to Salford which is the city right beside Manchester. I went for the interview and was told on the day that I had an unconditional place starting in February 1981. Just as well it wasn't dependent on my A Level results which were pretty unimpressive.

When I came out of hospital I moved in with Liz and her husband Craig who were expecting their first baby, Natalie. I had plaster casts on both feet up to my knees, and had to use crutches, so it was decided I needed to be "looked after." I never lived at home with Dad again after that. I moved straight from Liz's to the nurse's hall of residence in the grounds of Hope Hospital in Salford. I was on the tenth floor in one of two brand new tower blocks and I loved it.

9

Jobs

My first Saturday job was at the Wimpy Bar in Oldham. I can't remember how I got it and neither do I remember any kind of interview, but I do know I was thirteen and worked long hours. I think it was 9am-6pm on Saturdays. It started out as just waitressing but very quickly turned into me cooking the burgers and fries. It's hard to imagine that now. There was no training except by observing, no hygiene certificates and no health and safety rules. I fried the burgers and onions on a big flat plate and threw frozen chips in the fryer at an alarming rate. I learned how to make milk shakes, floats, teas and coffees and was paid £4.50 plus tips for the day – I thought I was rolling in money! After a while the guy running the place started to pay me a bit too much attention and I was desperate to get something else, by this time I was probably around fifteen years old. Saturday jobs were hard to come by and no one gave them up willingly. Again, I don't know how, but I got a job as a waitress in a café in the Tommyfield Market. It was owned by an older couple Margaret and George and I waited on tables as well as serving and making up sandwiches and soup. This was a big step up the salary scale as they paid me six pounds for the day. It was a small, busy café but there were about six of us on Saturdays including Margaret and George. I stayed there until I was seventeen when Mags, and her then husband, bought a hardware shop and I worked for them on Saturdays. They also paid me six pounds but it was so much easier. It wasn't busy like catering but I did have to sell paraffin by the gallon, screws and nails by the pound as well as all sorts of household cleaning and ironmongery – definitely a learning curve. Just having someone on the counter was a help for them and I spent some time, when there were no customers, revising for my A Levels. I remember having Tess of the d'Urbervilles and Chaucer out on the counter but clearly a D at A Level showed how little of it actually went in!

After that I left school and started nursing and then, unlike now in nursing, I earned a salary.

Having Saturday and holiday jobs definitely had a positive impact on my life on so many levels. It gave me money that I otherwise wouldn't have had which in turn enabled me to buy stuff that my peers had. There was little spare cash at home and as I previously said we had school uniform vouchers but the clothes you could get with them were so old fashioned and embarrassing to wear so I was able to buy more trendy clothes and shoes from the market. It also meant I could do some of the activities that my friends did or even go to the bakers for lunch instead of the dreaded free school dinners and the walk of shame without a "dinner ticket."

I babysat a lot for my siblings but didn't get paid for it in money. I did get board and lodgings and the comforts of more modern homes than I had with dad. Also, colour TV, central heating, different foods, as well as days out and holidays.

Most of the time there was extra work during the school holidays from the Saturday jobs so it wasn't unusual for me to be working full time even though I was still at school. There was no question of limiting hours for those underage or if there was, no one took any notice of it and thank goodness. The alternative was to have nothing or to get money from I don't know where. Fortunately, I always managed without resorting to anything dodgy! I think we were all brought up with a good work ethic and it's something I have tried to pass on, I believe successfully, to my own children. For all I hated maths and anything to do with it there were no electronic tills that told you how much change to give so there was no choice but to work it out and make sure it was correct. You were soon told by the punters if you didn't! When I think of the skills I learned from those jobs, not least resilience and independence, it makes me glad I did them. It wasn't always easy and I didn't always like getting up early or being on my feet all day and I'm sure it had an impact on my exam results at school. However, the alternative was not to be able to join in socially when my friends went out to discos or to have clothes that were not just unfashionable but downright awful! Socially I'm sure it helped me when I started nursing as I was already able to communicate well with adults that I didn't know. As I say, it gave me a good work ethos and I don't regret any of the jobs I did.

10

Going Out

Going out means different things at different stages of your life. Going out as a child largely meant playing outside close to home or venturing just a little further. It meant trips to the local library, neighbours, friends and the odd day out with whoever was around to take me anywhere.

As I got into my early and mid-teens "going out" took another turn that largely involved going out with friends. As I have said before we used to hang out a lot in Copster Hill Park but as we became more "sophisticated" we started going to discos. Obviously, this cost money both in admission and bus fares and I never asked dad for it. I funded it myself. It did mean I didn't have much left to spend on clothes which a lot of my peers did but at least I could go. There were under age discos in a few places and we did them all! Wednesday night was either Royton Assembly Hall or The Cat's Whiskers or "The Cats" as it was affectionately known and also Baileys which later became Romeo and Juliet's. They all finished at 10pm so the serious clubbers could get in! There was also Candlelight which was really for over eighteens and you had to lie about your age to get into that one. There were no ID checks, you just had to know your DoB and change the year accordingly. It was the same going to watch X films at the cinema. The irony was totally lost on us that we would get on the bus and claim to be under sixteen so we could pay a child's fare and then go upstairs, get the makeup on and get "dolled up" to get into the cinema. There were a lot of bus inspectors in those days and we were often challenged but, with the confidence of youth and the "right" date of birth there wasn't much they could do.

Once I started nursing Penny and I were frequent punters at Saturday's disco which was part of the old Britannia Hotel in Manchester. Again, we never had much money to spend so we rarely drank but we stayed until it closed (3am) to avoid bus or taxi fares back to the nurse's residence. We then just went straight to work at Salford Royal Hospital which is close to Manchester centre, the porters always let us in and we'd sleep for a couple of hours in the changing room until we started an early shift!

Sometimes Glynn, our nursing colleague, would take us to the gay club Heroes in Manchester and that was always a good night. We usually left him and his mates early because they would go off on their adventures to who knows where!

There were of course quite a few medics' parties that were pretty wild and often involved copious amounts of alcohol in a variety of cocktails – who says doctors are healthy? Both Penny and I had decided early on in our careers that we didn't want to be "one of those nurses" who only wanted to marry a doctor so we were massively underwhelmed by most of them, both parties and medics! Often when I was nursing in Salford, our local pub The Cross Keys would give us AT's (after time) which basically meant they shut the doors and carried on serving. Pubs were often "raided" by the police, looking for underage drinkers but again no one had ID and it was mostly used as a deterrent. The trick was always to have a soft drink in front of you so that if they asked, that's what you were drinking and you had no idea who that glass of cider belonged to!

Pubs played a big part in my early twenties and thirties, not least after I met Peter.

We were regulars in the Corstorphine Inn for many years before Paul and Suzy came along and we both had quite busy social lives through our respective works. Again, sometimes we got AT's which are more commonly called "lock-ins" in Scotland. Once I moved to Edinburgh, I didn't really go to discos so I wasn't particularly au fait with the clubbing scene here. I know Paul and Suzy both frequented The Hive and the Mission and I had many sleepless nights when it was "The Hive till Five"! I guess I conveniently forgot about my own dancing till dawn days as I berated them for being out all night! Sorry you two! I don't ever remember dad giving me a curfew when I lived at home but the expectation was that I was on the "last bus" which was at 10:30pm and I always was unless I particularly needed the money and then I'd walk home and save the bus fare!

When I think now of the anxieties from today's parents about what their children get up to, and to some extent my own when Paul and Suzy were growing up, I realise how much freedom we had. Most of us didn't have a house phone, much less a mobile phone, so you made the arrangements and stuck to them. We also didn't have easy access to cars and lifts so if you missed a bus then you had to walk home regardless of time or weather and then it usually meant getting a row if you were late. In the North West of England in the seventies we also grew up in the shadow of the infamous Moors Murderers as well as the Yorkshire Ripper across the Pennines. Although we didn't dwell too much on them, we were very aware of them and sometimes scared ourselves silly that they might be lurking around our home town.

11

Music and Gigs and TV Shows

Growing up in the seventies and eighties was an interesting era music wise. The Beatles were still well known but had split up by the time I was into music although both Eric and Liz were big Beatles fans. I was in the era of the first "boy bands," although I did like a few solo artists as well. Having quite an eclectic taste in artists my bedroom wall was covered in posters of David Bowie, Marc Bolan, The Sweet, Showaddywaddy, 10cc, ELO to name but a few. I didn't really get into the Osmonds who were a wholesome American family of singers and very much part of the music scene. However, my absolute pin up in my primary school and early secondary school years was David Cassidy! He was also on a sitcom on TV, The Partridge Family. I thought he was the "bee's knees" until the Bay City Rollers hit the scene and then I was sold. My affections turned along with millions of others. It was absolute hysteria at its best. They played Belle Vue in Manchester and I was desperate to go but dad refused to budge on it and I couldn't afford it anyway. Jenn and I scoured the Tommyfield Market for tartan remnants to sew down the sides of our jeans and make scarves. She loved Eric Faulkner but my favourite was Les McKeown. When I first met Peter, he told me that his sister Doreen was Les McKeown's first love when they were about five…they were in the same class at primary school. I couldn't believe it and I'm sure that's one of the reasons I continued to see him!

Top of the Pops was on TV the same night as First Aid and the dance troupe and the number one song was always last at 8pm; I remember Jennifer's dancing troupe teacher letting them all go home at 7:50pm so they would be in time to see them sing Bye Bye Baby and Shang a Lang, we never got to leave the First Aid class though, the Fentons were obviously a different age group than the dance troupe teacher!

Although I didn't think that I watched a lot of TV growing up I did watch some and writing this has made me realise that I probably watched more than I thought. TV wasn't a twenty-four-hour thing like it is today though and in my early years it wasn't possible to record anything so if you missed it, you missed it! Video recorders didn't really appear until I was in my early twenties and then it was a great treat to record something or to rent a movie to watch.

I didn't watch much at all until I was about seven because Grandma didn't have a set and we had the whole "money in the slot" situation going on at home. There also wasn't the range of kids' programmes that there is now. My early recollections of TV shows were Blue Peter, Animal Magic and Crackerjack with both Tiswas and Multi-Coloured Swap Shop on Saturday mornings. Apparently, Tiswas is an acronym for Today Is Saturday; Watch And Smile and was presented by Chris Tarrant and Sally James but I seem to remember Lenny Henry and Jasper Carrot being on some episodes too. I didn't know what Tiswas meant until I started writing this so…every day's a school day!

Multi Coloured Swap Shop was presented by Noel Edmunds who was also a Radio One DJ and someone I had a soft spot for. You could phone in and swap your toys and games there. Crackerjack was a chaotic Friday evening show that had games and quizzes and if the kids got an answer wrong, they were given a cabbage. Three cabbages and you were out! The winner of the quiz always got to choose a toy but everyone got a Crackerjack pencil and they were very sought after prizes a bit like the Blue Peter badge. I longed for a Blue Peter Badge or Crackerjack pencil but never got either. Apparently, our late queen Elizabeth managed to get Crackerjack pencils for Charles and Anne when she visited the studios but that was before I was born!

Most of what we watched in the evening was comedy or game shows. Grandma used to like Bruce Forsyth and the Generation Game and Dick Emery. A lot of the shows used to have a catch phrase so Brucie's was "Nice to see you, to see you nice!" and Dick Emery's was "Ooh you are awful, but I like you." Dad's Army was another favourite of Grandma's and Captain Mainwaring's phrase was always, "You stupid boy" to his young nephew played by Ian Lavender. Most of what was on back then seems really corny and very inappropriate now. Shows like the Black and White Minstrel Show, On the Buses and of course the whole series of "Carry On" episodes and films. It's hard to believe that these programmes that were full of sexism, misogyny and racism were so popular but they were and no one really challenged them apart from Mary Whitehouse who was a conservative activist and spoke out about the perils of social liberalism. She was a bit of a "marmite" person that divided opinion.

Another massively favourite programme for me was Starsky and Hutch which was a 70's American cop series starring Paul Michael Glaser (Starsky) and David Soul (Hutch). My friend Bernie and I were absolutely convinced we were going to marry this pair. Me Starsky and her Hutch! We never gave thought to how we were going to meet them let alone date and marry them when they lived in California and we lived in Oldham! We both had their posters up on our bedroom walls and I often stayed at Bernie's house up in her attic bedroom where we planned our future lives with David and Michael!

Coronation Street was another firm favourite of Gran's too that inevitably I ended up watching. When I was nursing at Salford Royal we sometimes had cast members come in for treatment because the hospital was so close to Granada Studios. It always caused a stir but we were sworn to secrecy even in as much as saying whether they were there or not.

We were never into movies: TV was seen as a short interlude and then it was switched off and we went on to do something else. Binge watching was also not an option and until the mid-seventies daytime TV wasn't even a thing.

When I was very young, before I went to school, Grandma and I would "Listen with Mother" on the radio after lunch. It was just a short story and a nice way to relax. I often fell asleep and so did Grandma but she always said she was "just resting her eyes". It must have been a short, welcome respite from the demands of a very feisty pre-schooler!

12

Relatives, Neighbours and Friends

My maternal grandmother came from a large family. She was the eldest followed by Uncles, Alf and Willie and Aunties, Margaret and Mary. Harry was her youngest brother (there had been another sibling, Hannah, but she died, long before I was born). Auntie Mary and Auntie Margaret lived together in the bungalow in Hampshire, Mary was a teacher and Margaret a nurse. I have no idea what took them south but, as far as I know, my great grandparents always lived in Lancashire. Uncle Alf and Uncle Willie both emigrated to New Zealand and married there. They often sent photos to Gran of their lives and it's a place that is still on my bucket list to see. Uncle Willie later divorced and moved back to the UK and remarried a lovely lady called Annie who was a great baker. Alf remained married to Zoe in New Zealand and I think both he and Auntie Margaret died when I was still living with Gran. After I met Peter and we went on holidays to France via Portsmouth, we would call in on Auntie Mary, latterly in a nursing home.

My mum, Mary Winterbottom, was the eldest of two, her younger brother being my Uncle Eric. It was his house that we lived in at Eldon Street. It's interesting how we have different memories of him. Mags remembers him as being a very prominent figure in her early years which was before he met his wife, Emily. Her memories are of him taking them into Manchester to see Father Christmas in one of the big department stores and buying them new clothes. I remember him as a more remote figure in my life. He was always generous with presents at birthdays and Christmas though. His wife Emily was older than him and was divorced which I think didn't sit well with Gran. She never said, but there was always a disapproving note to her voice when she spoke of either my dad or Emily. Maybe it was just a case of no one being good enough for her children to marry.

Dad had two younger siblings, John and Norah who had eleven children between them, ten girls and one boy. The children were all roughly ages with my siblings and they spent summers together over in Strangford where my dad was from. Apparently, he also had two older siblings who I knew nothing about until my cousin Patricia Kilgallon told me. Tommy who died at nine and Joe who died at twenty-one, we think of Tuberculosis (TB).

Strangford is a beautiful part of the world and sadly somewhere I have only been to once when Paul and Suzy were about five and three. My dad spoke very fondly of it all through my childhood and early years but would never go back once the "Troubles" started.

I am really only in touch with Patricia from Aunt Norah's family and through her I hear about her sisters. Their brother Alan died in recent years. On the Fitzsimons side I occasionally hear from my cousin Isobel and through both Patricia and Isobel and the power of Facebook I see the odd bits of extended family news.

My grandparents on dad's side were Nanna and Granda Fitzsimons who I think I only met once when I vaguely remember them coming to see us at Fir Tree Ave. Gran and Grandad Winterbottom, my mum's parents, were obviously closer in distance and Gran in particular, since Grandad died when I was about three, played a massive role in my life. They had owned a greengrocer's shop before I was born and Gran often spoke of it. I'm not sure if this was the only job granddad had or was something he did in his later years. Gran's maiden name was Leach but she became Sarah Winterbottom when she married and my brother Eric took great delight in calling her Sally Cowdbum (cold bottom!) which she took in good part if only because Eric could charm the birds off the trees!

It's only as you get older that you realise a lot of these memories will be lost forever which is why I'm writing them down now. I don't think for a minute that Paul and Suzy will have much interest in most of this until they're much older but by then I might not have the notion to write it. All I can say is stuff it in a box somewhere and come back to it whenever you want and if you don't want to, don't, but at least the option is there!

Neighbours played a big part in our lives especially when I lived on Eldon Street with Gran. It was very much a community and you could and did ask each other for help and it was given freely and graciously. There was a community spirit which although unspoken was very much around the old adage, "It takes a village to raise a child."

As I have said, if we were out playing and got hurt any number of neighbours would be on hand and likewise if you did something you shouldn't there were plenty of people to pick you up on it, and they did! You never complained at home if you'd been given a row by a neighbour because you'd be in more trouble for being cheeky! Our neighbours could be relied on though for impromptu childcare, borrowing grocery items, which were always replaced immediately, and general gossip and support. Neighbours would also shop for each other, particularly for the older people on the street especially if the weather was inclement. As I have said most neighbours on Eldon Street were given the titles "auntie and uncle" out of respect. This wasn't quite the same at home on Fitton Hill, where they were always Mr or Mrs and their surname and were somehow less prominent.

At home on Fir Tree Ave there were a lot of big families many of whom were Catholic and went to the local Catholic church and schools but not all. Many were Irish families but equally many weren't and everyone seemed to rub along fine in spite of the "troubles" across the water in Ireland.

Alice and Granville Mitchell were a massive part of my life when I moved from Eldon Street back home although Granville died when I was around seven. I was often to be found in their house in the evening after tea, partly for the company and partly because their house was so much warmer than ours!

There were particular local characters on Fitton Hill that everyone knew, Nobby Clark was the local police man who cycled around on his bike keeping law and order. Everyone loved his front garden which was full of gnomes and a wishing well! The local midwife, very respected in the community, lived next door to Dad and I when we crossed over to the dark side of the street at 118. We would sometimes watch her struggle to reverse her car out and after seeing her many failed attempts and near misses I was always glad that I never needed her services. I'm sure her midwifery skills were much better than her driving skills!

The church community was strong and dad was a regular at Holy Rosary for all the years we were on Fitton Hill up until he died. He was responsible for the offertory plate during the service, passing it round the pews to collect the money and then taking it up to the priest to be blessed and received. He was always very scathing of one of his officious "colleagues" and used to refer to him as The Bishop! It was the only time I ever really heard him take offence to anyone. The parish priest in my younger years was Father Buckley, a big gruff Irishman. I was always a bit scared of him because he would name and shame the boys at the back of the church if they messed around during the service. Again, no one took offence and the boys would no doubt get it again when they got home if they'd been disruptive. Mags remembers Father Buckley as a kind, gentle man but as I say I was a bit scared of him. Apparently, he was very good with our family when my mum died, which of course I don't remember.

There was an expectation that we went to Mass on Sunday although I have no idea how Dad would have reacted if we hadn't. I know the boys rebelled as teens and then left home and didn't go. Eric, Mags and Liz all had their children baptised Catholic whereas John and I didn't.

I went to church for years, until I left Fitton Hill, and then didn't go much at all after that. I'm not sure what, if anything, I got from it but it was a habit and believe it or not, in those days I wasn't rebellious at all and it just seemed to be what you did on a Sunday morning. Dad only went to evening Mass so I guess I could have said I'd been if I hadn't but I never did.

Neighbours became friends and the children, who by and large, went to the same local schools spent time socialising with each other. I'm pretty sure John and Eric had a thing with the two girls next door, in their teen years.

There were also other big families that my siblings hung out with by virtue of them just being around. The Higgins family next door but one was a large family and their father died around the same time as our mum I believe. Again, the siblings were the same ages as mine, so older than me, but I did play a lot with one of the grandchildren, Alison. We often sneaked off to Alexandra Park early in the morning, came home for dinner (lunch) and went back until teatime. No one came looking for us, no one really knew where we were, but the park was our garden and we loved it.

13

Places

Most places we went to in our younger days were local, apart from the holidays which have a whole section of their own. The rest of the time though we had neither money nor transport to go very far.

Alexandra Park was, and still is, a big park, although not as big as it seemed when we were young. There were so many different parts to it that we played in and hung out in. At the top end of the park near Abbey Hills which is where we lived until just before mum died were the big, white, stone lions that are still there.

Lions at Alexandra Park

Always good for a climb up and there was a covered area behind them which was useful for sheltering in from the rain! In the middle between the lions and boating pond were two huge shiny rocks that we all climbed on top of and slid down. They could be anything from a mountain to a ship in our imaginations.

Then there was also the bowling green which was probably the place we avoided most because it was very strict and you had to have special shoes to go on it and the old men got grumpy if you walked on it. The tennis courts and crazy golf were usually too expensive and the park was policed very effectively by the park keepers who kept a close eye out for anyone who went on without paying or who was misbehaving. The rest of the park was free though and there were two playgrounds with swings, slides and roundabouts, lots of gardens and the big field to play on as well as the greenhouses and the "monkey steps" which took you down to the entrance closest to Fitton Hill.

Copster Hill Park and Werneth Park were also places we hung out in as I got older and went to senior school. They were both significantly smaller parks but the catchment for St. Anselm's was much wider and we tended to hang out closer to school. Some of my friends came from the opposite end of Oldham and even Failsworth which seemed a long way away then but in reality, it isn't. School was pretty much equidistant for us all so we migrated around there. Occasionally we went into Manchester but not very often. We had no money to spend if we did and it seemed a waste of two bus fares each way.

Tandle Hill Park in Royton close to where my brother John and his family still live, was another place we sometimes went to but again, usually if we had to pay to get there i.e. bus fares, we didn't bother.

The Tommyfield Market was always good for a mooch around but it was only open on Fridays and Saturdays and most Saturdays I was working. When I worked in the market, I would sometimes go on my lunch break looking for bargains and planning what I'd buy with my well-earned wages.

Bury Market was another big north of England market and was also where Uncle Willie and Auntie Annie lived. Grandma and I would sometimes go there on Saturday and then go to their house for tea which was always worth a visit because Annie was a great baker. Bury is also where Uncle Eric lived for a while and is still where my good friend Bev from nursing days lives. The market remains open and Mags and her husband Robert occasionally go. It's famous for its black puddings which are something I used to eat as a child but not anymore! It's sad that a lot of the old markets are no longer there, they were always a source of fresh fruit and vegetables at good prices as well as cheap clothes and household items. The big supermarkets now have the monopoly and their stuff is definitely not as good or as local.

We have always had a theatre in Oldham, the Coliseum, which has recently been saved from closure due to public outcry. The building dates back to 1885 and is a source of pride in the town. A number of celebrities have come through Oldham Coliseum including a few from Coronation Street, Emmerdale and Brookside. Other performers include Charlie Chaplin, Ralph Fiennes and Minnie Driver. We were sometimes taken there from school, especially in exam years to watch the relevant plays related to our set books. I remember seeing Twelfth Night and King Lear as well as the Full Monty which was definitely not part of our Catholic school curriculum!

Oldham Swimming Baths was another place we occasionally went to with Grandma, as I said earlier, for her regular Friday afternoon bath but sometimes for a swim, me not Grandma! It was an old building and the changing rooms were around the edge of the pool and some on an upper balcony overlooking the pool.

We were also taken swimming from school when I was at Holy Rosary and the whole class (35+) would walk down to catch the 409 bus into town with just our class teacher. When I think now of the risk assessments we have to do as teachers today and the ratios of staff to children even to go around the local area there is no comparison. The pool itself was quite small and at that stage I couldn't swim so it wasn't my favourite place. I had to keep one leg on the bottom of the pool to stay afloat! It was always something different though and I was grateful to be taken. Eventually the old building was pulled down and a shiny new pool built but I never used it as by that time I had left Oldham.

Blackpool and Southport were occasional day trip destinations on the coach. I loved going to both but I was always terribly travel sick even though it wasn't that far. It seemed like a long drive but it probably wasn't much more than an hour. Eric also used to take me too, usually in a car but it made no difference. I was still very sick. It was all soon forgotten though when we got there until we had to face the return journey. I think it's something I passed on to Paul as he was also awfully travel sick as a young child.

Me and Eric at Southport

Oldham rugby at Watersheddings, which was Oldham's rugby league ground, was a place I frequented as a teenager. At this point, Eric played for Oldham so he sometimes got free tickets for me and a friend. He was often in the local paper; the Oldham Chronicle (Chron) and I lived in his reflective glory, soaking up the attention he got. After playing he moved into coaching and assistant coaching jobs in Oldham, Sheffield, Whitehaven, Rochdale and Bramley. He was quite well known in the rugby league world and was often featured in the Oldham Chron as a local hero. He also coached Rugby Union at Ashton and Rochdale as well as some smaller clubs.

Watersheddings was a draughty old place and was always bitterly cold. Apart from Eric though, I had the whole thing of the school rugby captain going on who later became the captain of Oldham so I suffered the cold and rain but it never did get me a date with him!

14

The Salford Years

I started nursing in February 1981 in Salford, and officially moved out of Oldham into the nurse's residence. I couldn't believe my luck when I saw my accommodation: small but cosy, my rent came out of my salary before I got it, and included all bills except food. I thought I was rich...I was in comparison to what little money I had earned while at home. I'd had Saturday jobs from being thirteen, first in the Wimpy Bar, then in a café in the Tommyfield market and finally in Mags and her then husband's shop, an ironmongers.

First night in the accommodation I met my neighbours. Ann Marie who was also from my home town fifteen miles away, a girl from Glasgow and a girl more local to Salford. Neither of the latter two finished the course but Ann Marie and I did and were friends throughout. We're still in touch today although we rarely meet. The fifth and final person on the corridor was a second-year nurse who had the most spectacular rows with her boyfriend. He unofficially lived there but they were always rowing with each other and when she played "Love Don't Live Here Anymore" by the American band Rose Royce, we knew it was all "temporarily" off!

Both Mags and Liz had their second babies, Laura and Gareth, while I was nursing and so my days off were spent visiting them, sadly less so Gran and Dad who didn't compete well with the "cute" factor of new babies.

Gran died in the nursing home after having a brain haemorrhage, she was ninety-two. I wish I had been there more in her later years than

I was, it was only after having children myself I realised how hard it must have been for someone in their seventies and eighties to bring up a young child. She would also have been grieving her daughter and husband's deaths within three years of each other. What a woman: strong willed, determined, resilient. I hope both me and Suzy have inherited some of her traits...I think we have.

After six weeks in nurse school at Peel House in Salford we were assigned our first hospital and ward to work on. I was to be based at Salford Royal which was actually closer to Manchester City Centre than Salford. It was very close to the Granada Studios and we occasionally had celebrities from the Coronation Street set coming to use the facilities! My first ward was S2 -male surgical specialising in Genito Urinary surgery...lots of prostates!

The S2 team were a good team, albeit the two ward sisters a bit aloof and scary. The other students and staff nurses really looked after me. We were expected to clean the sluice, including bedpans, as well as nurse and had been thoroughly taught how to bed bath patients, make beds, carry out wound dressings and give injections into an orange.... all very well until we met the real thing.

My first injection was a nerve-wracking experience and not helped by the poor old gentleman who was as thin as a stick and yelled at the top of his voice that he was having, "No student nurse sticking a needle into me."

He wanted the staff nurse or sister nothing less. A rather large gentleman in the next bed offered to let me give him his injection saying he had a big target to practise on, the injection was duly done, we both survived! After the second one I was a pro and I still remember being told, draw an imaginary cross over the buttock, use the upper right quadrant, taut the skin and stick it in. We all had the fear that if we didn't draw the imaginary line, we would hit the sciatic nerve and that would not be good, either for us or the patient. Fortunately, I gave hundreds of injections after that and never once hit the sciatic nerve...phew!

Dressings were saved for the afternoon because most of the surgery was done in the morning and it was just too busy escorting patients to and from theatre and doing pre and post op observations (blood pressure, pulse, temperature and respirations). The sisters made sure things ran like clockwork and they did. We had a great team including a fantastic ward clerk, who did all the paperwork and two cleaners who did a lot more than clean. But clean they did: floors, worktops, locker tops and window sills. They changed patient's water jugs, made cups of tea and would often give a kind word and even a cuddle to a patient or student nurse who'd had a hard day. We lost a lot when the domestic services were tendered out and the cleaners were no longer attached to a team. I don't think it's a coincidence that hospital acquired infections have risen considerably since. The cleaners were always an integral part of the team and came on nights out with us all. Now you're lucky to see the same person twice and it's not their "job" to do so many things we took for granted.

Back to dressings...

In nurse training school we had been taken through the "aseptic technique" by our very strict tutor, Imelda Jenkins. We had four tutors in total Ann Edwards, Jessie Evans, Tom Le Grande and Imelda Jenkins, who was by far the scariest.

Standards were high and you were told in no uncertain terms when you didn't reach them. First you had to prepare the area (surgical trolley on wheels) by washing it with warm water and then an alcohol wipe. Then, after scrubbing your own hands, you got a dressing pack and opened it out onto the trolley. This bit was tricky because you had to use the tips of your fingers to open the tight pack with as little contact as possible. Once in you could retrieve the forceps and then adeptly, (eventually!) use them to set out your "stall". Two mini pots, one for saline solution for cleansing and one with Savlodil which was a Savlon type solution for killing any germs. There were cotton wool balls and a gauze dressing, none of which were to make contact with your hands. Everything was carried out using the tweezer like forceps. A daunting procedure for a new student who'd only been a nurse for six weeks, even more daunting when I found out what I had to dress...penises!

I thought it was a joke until the staff nurse told me it wasn't. Today, I could observe but after that I would be "on" dressings in the afternoon and I'd just have to get on with it. And so, it came to be that for eight weeks I spent most afternoons putting dressings around men's penises. They had all had prostatectomies and had urethral catheters which I was told needed dressed daily to keep infection at bay. This meant swabbing said penis with saline solution, followed by Savlodil and then wrapping gauze around it at the entry point of the catheter...with forceps. Once the tip was covered you could then use your hands to tape it in place... no gloves in those days! I learnt quickly to have the tape cut up ready on the trolley so that the whole procedure could be finished without too much fuss. I also learned how to fasten it, just enough to stay on but not strong enough to have to spend any period of time unpicking sticky tape off a catheter and penis, when the dressing was to be re done the following day. I was nineteen, naïve and with a Catholic upbringing, it was a whole new world!

My first ward was a massive learning curve but I loved it. I loved the uniform, even the hat with one blue band around it to show I was a first year. I learned how to change intravenous infusions, dress other wounds as well as penises and do a medicine round with a trained member of staff. The teaching was excellent both on and off the ward. We were visited regularly by clinical tutors; another dragon of a woman was Miss Critchley who would pounce at any given moment and ask you to work through a procedure with her. Bed baths were her favourite and you had to make sure you started in the right place, changed the water at the right time and could make a bed efficiently with a patient still in it. It took most of the morning and the ward sisters hated it because effectively they were a member of staff down. Students were very much part of the work force and we were taught very effectively on the job, the motto being, "See one, Do one, Teach one."

After S2 it was back into "school" for two weeks then a medical rotation. I got WM2 which was female medical and not nearly as much fun as surgical I thought. There were a lot of diabetics and heart attacks and it was where I came across my first death, an elderly lady. I remember the ward sister saying we would lay her out together. We washed the body, (another bed bath) and dressed her in a clean gown. The sister was kind and respectful to both me and the dead lady. When we had finished, she took a Gideon Bible out of the locker, (there was one in every locker donated by the Gideon Society in those days) opened it a random page and then went off to find a single flower which she laid delicately across the open bible. It was a lovely touch and something I always did after that whenever I laid someone out. Not sure it would be appropriate now and it's unlikely there would be bibles in the lockers but I know many relatives passed comment on the gesture and drew comfort from it.

Second Year

Back into nursing school after medicine, and then a double rotation – eight weeks in paediatrics followed by eight weeks in Geriatrics, now Care of the Elderly. I was on the paediatric oncology (cancer) ward which was tough but rewarding and I learned so much. The hospital was The Royal Hospital for Sick Children or Pendlebury as it was fondly called because of its location in that area of the city. It was, and still is, a Centre of Excellence, although it's no longer at Pendlebury, and the teaching was second to none. We had nine deaths in eight weeks which was heartbreaking but the staff were incredible. We were treated much more like students at Pendlebury, I guess because of the nature of children's nursing and the particular ward. The trained staff, thankfully, did most dressings and certainly end of life care. We were very much part of the team though. I enjoyed my time but had no desire to go back, strange considering I went on to do my sick kids training after I'd completed my adult training. More of that later.

Geriatrics was in a very old purpose built (early 20th century!) hospital called Ladywell. It was a very different experience and a much slower pace. A lot of our time was spent on basic nursing care which was good training. The only downside was that geriatrics was one of Imelda Jenkins' favourite specialities and she was always around the wards looking for teaching opportunities to drum into us. As we got further into training though she did soften a little and was actually quite funny once you'd proved your worth. So, geriatrics took us to the end of first year and our second year beckoned.

Second year had started with another period in school before heading to an eight-week rotation on nights followed by four weeks each of obstetrics and community.

I enjoyed nights, the first-time round. I was partnered up with a girl from my class, Penny, who became a great friend for many years after. We were allocated to a female medical ward that specialised in renal problems and neuro medicine as well as general medical conditions. Penny had completed two nights of her first week by the time I came in for my first. She informed me it was "just us" – there was a Sister or Nursing Officer (NO) on duty for all the medical wards but most of the time we would be left to our own devices. The Sister or NO would come round after we had had "handover" from the day staff. At some point before "lights out" we had to do a drug round with them. Just like the other procedures we were taught meticulously and as students couldn't administer drugs without a trained nurse. We also had to be assessed and this included knowledge of the drug, dose, use and side effects. It was quite daunting. After that the Sister/NO would go on her "rounds" to the other wards and it was our job to settle the patients ready for bed. That could mean toileting, washing patients, taking and recording observations: Blood Pressure, Temperature, Pulse and Respirations. Also looking after any intravenous infusions (drips) and making sure they were running properly. Once the lights were out that's when the fun started...or not. As we all know when we feel unwell it's worse at night and we had some very sick patients. Penny and I were still only a year into our training but we were the only ones there. Sometimes we had an auxiliary nurse with us who was basically an untrained nurse. Usually, they had been there for years and their experience and knowledge were invaluable. We all dreaded a "crash call" which was a medical emergency and one where you didn't hang about. There was a big button on the wall in the office and if you pressed it a whole team hurtled through the ward with the "crash trolley," a big cart with the defibrillator machine and emergency drugs.

We had a couple of crash calls on nights and it never got easier. It wasn't all gloom and doom though. We had some real laughs and some incredible patients. We had to sit right in the middle of the long "Nightingale" ward and regularly check all the patients. The Sister/NO would come at some point and we had to take them around each bed telling them: name, age, diagnosis and treatment for each patient – without notes. It didn't matter if you had only had a handover a couple of hours before you were expected to know it. One night I had gone for "lunch" and Penny fell asleep on her chair in the middle of the ward. A lovely patient called Mary heard the Sister's heels coming down the corridor and, in an effort to save Penny from a good telling off, started to throw things off her locker to wake her up and distract the Sister. It worked and she claimed confusion from a bad dream that had made her throw the contents of the locker into the centre of the ward! Eight weeks of nights were enough and it would be a whole year before we had to do them again.

I loved obstetrics, my next placement, especially the labour ward where I saw lots of babies being delivered. Again, as students we observed a lot and weren't directly responsible for most procedures, thank goodness. I really enjoyed the post-delivery ward where you could help new mums with their babies too. I wasn't daunted by this like some of my fellow students as I'd had a lot of practise being an auntie.

Community was a totally different experience and was a mixture of district nursing, health visiting and clinics. It was a whole new world. Salford was then quite a deprived area and we visited patients across the whole social spectrum. Again, I had some fantastic teachers and some interesting visits. A health visitor and I turned up for a "first visit" which happened on day ten of the baby's life; the earlier days being the midwife's domain. We knocked at the door and were greeted by a lovely African lady who said her husband and baby were in bed. We went through to the living area and true to her word the husband was lying on a bed settee, stark naked cuddling the baby. The health visitor never missed a beat, greeted him as though it was the most normal thing in the world and asked to check the baby over. I wasn't sure where to put myself but she nodded toward the portable scales and told me to set them up. She briskly took the baby and proceeded to undress him. When we got to the nappy stage, terry towelling in those days, no disposables, she whisked it off and we both took a sharp intake of breath. The nappy was covered in blood but the child wasn't bleeding and seemed perfectly happy. When the health visitor asked what had happened the father said, "Oh, we circumcised him last night."Apparently, this was normal practice in their culture and they didn't think there was a problem. To be fair the health visitor checked the baby over, suggested a trip to the GP and baby clinic later in the afternoon to get "double checked" by the doctor and we were off. She never judged or was disrespectful and they duly arrived later with a happy baby. The GP, satisfied that the job had been done correctly, sent them on their way. The health visitor explained that community-based nursing was all about building relationships. If you went into someone's home you were a guest and you had to earn their trust and respect. Most of the time that paid off but as a Health Visitor myself, later on in my career, there were times when you did have to lay down the law – literally!

The people of Salford and surrounding areas were generally kind, friendly, salt of the earth folk. They didn't have much but they almost always made you welcome. The area I was in had a large Asian community, many of whom had arrived from India and Pakistan with the promise of new lives and jobs. They worked hard and were always polite and visiting them always resulted in some goody bag or treat that they insisted on giving you. Usually, if Indian, home-made sweets or sticky dessert. If Pakistani, often curry or samosas and it would have been very rude to refuse! As a health visitor particularly, as I found out later, you had a lengthy relationship with a family, until the child went to school. Obviously, if younger siblings followed you could be visiting a family for years and if they had elderly parents that was also a remit we had too.

My final year as a student was divided up between an eight-week placement in a psychiatric hospital (Prestwich) a stint of nights which I did on a Male Surgical Ward this time at Hope Hospital, followed by a speciality rotation onto neurosurgery and an eight-week placement shared between Accident and Emergency and Theatres.

We had to move halls of residence for the psychiatric placement as the Prestwich Hospital was self-contained and we didn't have transport. Prior to this we had moved out of the tower block into a lovely old house that was owned by the hospital. Oakwood was only for third year students. I loved it but Ann Marie hated it and wanted to move into a more modern house which she did.

Back to Prestwich...

I was on a female medium to long stay ward which I enjoyed. It was very sad though as a number of the women had been in there for years just because they had had a child out of wedlock or some other minor misdemeanour. Others suffered with schizophrenia and various other mental health issues. The psychiatric nurses were definitely a different breed from general nurses. The charge nurses and sisters were much more laid back and less concerned with overpowering routines. Visiting times were flexible, so unlike the general wards, there could be visitors at any time. Most of my cohort were on "Admission" wards which was crisis management for suicide attempts and other acute psychiatric emergencies. They had a very different experience from me. I enjoyed my time there and seriously considered the post registration psychiatric nursing course when I finished but I decided against it because it was an eighteen-month course and I'd had enough of studying.

The medium/long stay ward had been home for almost all the patients for a long time. Some for many years. As such it was treated as their home. They had their own rooms with their possessions and small furnishings in and the staff often put on entertainment for them or took them out around the village to the shops. There were some characters though. One old lady who was tiny, definitely under five feet, and had no teeth, had a penchant for taking all her clothes off and running around the village. For some reason she often did it in the Oxfam shop and we would get regular phone calls to come and collect her. The charge nurse, an affable Irish man, probably only in his late twenties, who in spite of being mortified at some of her lewd comments and behaviour, would set out with one of us students and a big winter coat to cover her dignity and bring her back! Likewise, another lady, who tested his good nature to the limits, would flush her bra down the toilet, flooding the communal bathrooms and causing chaos! As a student I enjoyed it but it couldn't have been the ideal place for these women who lived there for years. In the late eighties many of the long-term residents were rehoused in small group settings. I often wondered how they managed after being institutionalised for so long.

I had an on/off relationship with one of the male psychiatric nurses who had actually joined our general course. It fizzled out after a few months and although at the time I was pretty upset I never really thought it would last.

Back at Salford Royal I went into Accident and Emergency (A&E). I loved it. It was fast paced, exciting, upsetting and very rewarding all at once. Although we certainly had "regulars," characters who came back for various reasons, we didn't have the problems and violence that are such common features of life in A&E today. Neither did we have the same number of drug and alcohol related problems that are often the cause of the violence today.

Everyone was part of the team: doctors, students, nurses, porters and technicians.

This was especially true when the "red phone" rang. This was the emergency phone which was linked directly to ambulance control and always signalled a serious emergency. Salford Royal, as I said previously, was almost in Manchester City Centre and much closer than Manchester Royal Hospital and so we had our fair share of emergencies. Often road traffic accidents, home accidents, heart attacks and strokes. Sometimes suicide attempts, but never stabbings or gunshot wounds and rarely drug related incidents. How times have changed.

Theatre came next and I can't say it was my favourite place, especially not "Neuro Theatre." This dealt with brain and spinal surgery and the surgeons were absolutely ahead of their time. Salford was one of the leading areas for neurosurgery in the whole country. The precision and patience involved was incredible and it wasn't unusual for a case to start at the beginning of our shift and still be ongoing when we, as nurses, were finished. It was boring and tiring though as there was nothing to see, no screens for viewing in those days and you had to be quiet all the time so the surgeon could concentrate. I did my theatre rotation with a friend from my nursing cohort, Glyn. He was an absolute riot. Very proud and irreverent about his "gay" status and poked fun at himself as much as others. Many times, I had to turn my back or leave the room to stop myself laughing at some of his antics. He was an excellent nurse and a great friend. I shared a house with him and his friend just after I qualified. He would take Penny and I to the gay night clubs in town and we had some really good nights, particularly at Heroes which was his favourite haunt. He also loved to keep people guessing about his sexuality and took great delight in throwing out red herrings about who we were all partners with. In truth we were all just friends. Sadly, Glyn died from AIDS in Switzerland, where he lived with his partner in the early 90's.

Towards the end of our training, it became obvious that we were on the Nursing Officer's radar for jobs that might be coming up. Salford Royal was a small hospital, Hope Hospital larger and so more of my cohort were based at Hope. I knew I preferred surgery to medicine and although I had enjoyed some of the specialities, I also knew I didn't want to work in any of them, particularly at first.

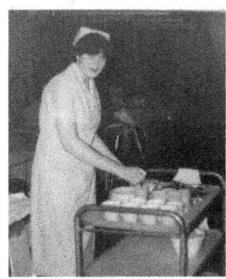

Me in my nurse's uniform

I was absolutely delighted when a job came up on S1 which was Female Surgery and Gynaecology. I loved it and went there for my final placement and couldn't believe my luck when I got the Staff Nurse job there. The team was amazing and I have a couple of lifelong friends who I worked with, namely Bev McAllister and Jayne Handley. The ward was busy and always full. There were several surgeons who had patients on there and they were true gentlemen. All men at that time. I learned so much on S1 not just about nursing but also about working as a team, leadership skills and relationships. Even so I only stayed for fifteen months because I had decided I would take the next step in my career and do my sick children's nursing.

15

The Green Goddess and Other Modes of Transport

We never had a car while I was growing up, in fact I'm not even sure my dad could drive. We managed perfectly with "Shanks Pony' (walking!) or on the bus. The bus service was good in and around Oldham and as I say the bus stop from town was right outside our house. We mostly walked though, and didn't think too much of it. Sometimes in my teens I would walk home from town late at night to save the bus fare, although growing up in Oldham we had been brought up to be wary of walking home alone. We were reasonably close to Saddleworth Moor where the "Moors Murderers" had carried out their atrocities. Likewise, we were only a stone's throw from Yorkshire where the Yorkshire Ripper carried out his atrocities too.

The Green Goddess

A few of my friends, Bernie in particular, learned to drive when we were still at school and she sometimes got to borrow her mum's Fiesta. I had to wait until I started nursing and was earning money to pay for driving lessons, they were a lot of money then, £6 each! I learned with a guy called Arthur who had taught my sister, Liz. I used to go to Eric's house to pick up my lesson because it was half way from Salford where I was living and Oldham where Arthur lived. Around this time Craig (Liz's husband) was selling his old Ford Escort – a black one that he'd used for rallying! I bought it from him, I thought

I was the "Bees Knees" except most of the time I couldn't start it. I failed my first driving test when Arthur didn't turn up to take me – he forgot! Eric's neighbour took me to the test centre in the Escort but I think the examiner took one look at me and then the car and decided neither of us should be on the road! I got six free lessons from Arthur after that to make up for his mistake but I still failed test two. I eventually passed but still had trouble starting the Escort! Enough was enough. I'd spent a fortune on parts and had ended up in debt so decided to sell it. At the time Penny had a Honda 70cc moped that she was selling. I bought it and loved it. It was a lovely blue colour and so cheap to run, so reliable after the Escort and so easy to park. After a year or so I traded it in for "The Green Goddess." This was another Honda but this time 90cc a real mean machine! It was also green, hence its name, and you could see me coming from miles away!

I could get to and from Oldham, Salford and the surrounding areas to see my dad and siblings for pennies. I suppose I had youth on my side and I never felt unsafe or worried about riding my Hondas. I only came off once when it was icy and I very elegantly slid sideways at a set of traffic lights on Manchester Rd heading up to Oldham. It did shake me up a bit though and it wasn't long after that I started to look for another car.

Eventually, I bought a Triumph Dolomite from my old school friend Angela Clarke who was also a nurse but in Oldham. That was a decent reliable car but it didn't capture my heart in the way that "Jessi car" did. Jessi car was an old orange, VW Beetle. I bought her from one of the girls on my nursing course for £99. I had her for a year and sold her for £100! I think it was the only car I've ever made a profit on.

After that I bought the Fiat Panda that was an absolute work horse and took me up and down to Edinburgh, although Peter always referred to it as a "biscuit tin on wheels!" He hated it so much he gave me the surprise of my life the

The Fiesta Firefly

first Christmas in Edinburgh and bought me a brand-new red Fiesta Firefly. I loved that car.

16

Booth Hall – Sick Kids Nursing

I applied for the sick children's nursing course at Great Ormond Street, London, Birmingham Children's Hospital and Booth Hall in Manchester – not the same hospital I had done my eight-week rotation in during my second year. I got into all three. Everyone assumed I'd choose Great Ormond St but I didn't. I don't know why; it just didn't feel right and neither did Birmingham. I settled for Booth Hall and moved to North Manchester to share a house with Penny. By this time Penny was engaged to a soldier who had fought in the Falklands and was still on active service. We didn't last long in the house; the landlord was creepy and "moved in" with us. Penny decided to go back home to save for her wedding as her parents lived locally. I didn't know what to do as I didn't fancy being in the house with "Creepy Alan." That's when Glyn came to the rescue and offered me a room in his house.

We had such fun times there. Glyn got more and more outrageous around his sexuality and decided he would move to Switzerland and then Amsterdam. He got jobs easily, as I said earlier, he was a good nurse. I stayed in the house for a couple of months but then Ann Marie was looking for a house mate and I moved into a rented terraced house first with her and then the same house with another friend Cath Byrne.

I can't say I loved my sick kids training. I felt the staff were very cliquey, but I was determined to finish and I did. We were a mixed group and obviously because we already had our general training, we were all at different stages of our careers. I met a lifelong friend, Diane, who was actually a Nursing Officer on the Children's Unit at Birch

Hill Hospital in Rochdale. In spite of many years' experience she had to have the sick kids' qualification. She was a fantastic nurse and teacher as well as a great mentor and friend. She never once pulled rank or used her status to undermine any of the people who were her bosses or colleagues throughout the training. We had some good times and she certainly kept everything in perspective. I never considered quitting but I didn't overly enjoy it either and Diane definitely kept me on the straight and narrow. I'm still in touch with her and she is now in her eighties!

The best placement by far was at St Mary's Hospital in Manchester on the Special Care Baby Unit. (SCBU). The babies were so tiny and it was very demanding physically and mentally. The hospital was a real Centre of Excellence for the North West of England and sick neonates were brought from all over, as far as Lancaster and Blackpool area as well as south Manchester and Cheshire. Often babies were flown in by air ambulance and it was a very traumatic time for the families. Many times, the mum was left in the birth hospital if she was too unwell to travel and the partner was faced with who to visit, the baby or the mother and often there were other children at home too. Some of the babies were in the unit for months. Often, they weighed less than a bag of sugar when they arrived and they ran into all sorts of problems and crises. It was a long haul for some families and sadly some of the babies didn't make it.

17

More Holidays and The One That Changed My Life!

Nurse training, when I did it in the eighties, was very different from now. Student nurses were part of the workforce and we earned a salary. Our academic training was carried out in the School of Nursing attached to each Health Authority. We weren't strictly students like university students. The salary seemed like a lot of money to me and it was in comparison to anything I'd earned before from "Saturday" jobs. My accommodation (at Salford) was taken directly from my salary and this meant I only had food and my own expenses to spend my money on; I was therefore able to go away on holiday several times.

Penny had a car and a tent and we had quite a few weekends camping in North Wales which was pretty close to us, just a couple of hours away. We also spent a few weekends up north at Liz and Craig's house not far from Glasgow in a small village called Chapelton. We even got stuck there once because we got snowed in.

We had "set" holidays during nurse training at Salford so rather like school holidays we had no control over when they were. One of the times, I went to Ibiza with Ann Marie, and another time I went on a camping holiday to France with my good friend Bev from Ward S1, to the same place we went to years later with our babies, Paul and Ross.

The holiday that changed my life though came in the middle of my Sick Kids training at Booth Hall. Here we were post registration students and had more flexibility about choosing when we took our holidays.

I had lost touch with Penny at this point (she was engaged to the guy in the army who served in the Falklands War). We weren't working in the same place anymore which made it harder to stay in contact, no mobile phones then. Her fiancé was still posted overseas so Penny had arranged their wedding and honeymoon and then changed her mind!

She phoned me one day to ask if I had any holidays to take and would I want to go away on holiday with her. She had cancelled an exotic honeymoon but the travel agent had told her she only had the option of a week in Majorca within the next month or she would lose all her money. I had just come out of a rocky relationship with a pharmacist and thought it was a great idea. Neither of us had any interest in another relationship and thought a "girly" holiday was just what we needed.

We flew from Manchester Airport into Majorca, our destination – Magaluf. Paul and Suzy cringe when they hear this as it has had a reputation for its wild nightclub and bar culture amongst other things!

Our hotel was very nice and we had half board which meant what money we had, which wasn't a lot really, could be spent on nights out. We decided, sensible as we were, not to drink too much but just enjoy the clubs and we also decided to designate each night to drinking only one type of drink so we didn't mix drinks and end up shitfaced! Sometimes I surprise myself at how sensible we were...or not! First night was gin night and we had a great time. We arrived back at the hotel just in time for a shower before breakfast and then we slept on the beach and around the pool all day! The second night was wine night. We had dinner and headed out. After a few drinks we arrived at "Alexandra's Disco" which was one of the nightclubs on the island. We hadn't been in long when Penny told me there was a guy at the bar that I would like! I told her I wasn't interested after the whole pharmacist fiasco. She said he was my type, dark hair, moustache and a white shirt. Her type was men in uniforms and even though she'd just got rid of one she eventually married another, a policeman! At some point we got chatting to the "guy," Peter and his brother, Roy. They were good company but we never thought too much about it. After that we bumped into them a few times but they were going home to Edinburgh a couple of days before our holiday ended. Peter and I swapped phone numbers – no mobiles then so no texts! I didn't expect to hear from him. Penny hadn't exchanged numbers with Roy. When Peter phoned me a couple of times over the next few weeks, I still didn't think too much of it, Edinburgh was a long way away! The next time he phoned however he said he was going to visit his uncle in Leicester and could he stop by on the way, maybe go out for dinner? He came and we had a long chat. He was married but had separated and was living with his brother Roy. Like me he hadn't expected to meet anyone and wasn't sure how or where it would go. We thought we would take things slowly. He went off to Leicester and after the first visit either he came to Manchester most weekends or I went to Edinburgh on my days off. It was the start of a very long-term relationship and my life in Edinburgh!

18

Early Days in Edinburgh

It was a big move and yet with the combination of the naivety of youth and being lovestruck it didn't seem that big at all. I was twenty-four, had a permanent new job, a boyfriend and somewhere to live. What else did I need?

I had been driving up and down to Edinburgh in my Fiat Panda for months in my "biscuit tin on wheels" as Peter rudely called it! Anyway, I packed it up with everything I owned and drove North. I'm not sure what my family really thought of it at all. As I said previously, Dad was a very unassuming man and didn't interfere with any decisions we made. I hadn't lived at home since I was seventeen and he had obviously got used to my infrequent, impromptu visits so it didn't really matter whether I was coming to see him from Manchester or Edinburgh.

My siblings were all busy with jobs and homes and very young families. Interestingly, Liz and Craig had moved to Scotland for a while prior to this and had lived on the outskirts of Glasgow for a couple of years. I had spent a lot of time there with them and had also gone with Penny. They however moved back to England before I moved to Scotland.

Early days at Corstorphine Hill Ave

I think there were a few raised eyebrows from some family and friends that Peter was twelve years older than me and already had a family. Michelle was fifteen and Stewart twelve, but no one tried to stop me and it wouldn't have worked if they had. I moved into Roy's house and we fell into a routine of work and pub and not much else. Peter and I decided quite quickly that we needed our own space and set about looking for a mortgage and then at flats to buy. We were lucky, it was a time when it wasn't difficult to get a 98% or even a 100% mortgage and we seemed to get one relatively easily. We started looking at flats. I was horrified. Edinburgh was expensive. Back in the north west of England it was possible to get a 3 bedroomed terraced house for under £15,000, in Edinburgh that wouldn't get us a one bedroomed flat. We looked at quite a few before Peter told me we had a viewing for a flat up Corstorphine Hill. We went to view; I couldn't believe it. It was awful!

Every room except the bathroom was turquoise blue, including the front door. The bathroom was a "lovely" salmon pink with towelling curtains of the same shade. There was no central heating, it needed to be re-plumbed and rewired. Peter thought it was amazing. He had  already planned in his head how and what he was going to do with it. I remember standing in the hall thinking how can we possibly even think of buying this? But we did, it cost us £32,000 and my family and friends thought we were mad. Peter was delighted, he loves a project. He and Roy, both gas fitters by trade, started by putting in central heating. They were well known especially in the local pub where there was a massive pool of tradesmen to recruit to help, in exchange for servicing fires and boilers and central heating or other manual work. They were both excellent tradesmen and saved us a fortune. People in the pub were also kind and we found ourselves the recipients of a suite, fridge and washing machine that were being upgraded by various friends. We were delighted to have them, as money was tight, and by March we had moved into a newly plumbed, rewired and centrally heated flat. Hard to believe that we hadn't even known each other for a year! We renovated the flat bit by bit, both of us working overtime to raise funds. Once we moved in, I saw the potential that Peter had seen in it. It had amazing views at the back over the Pentland Hills and our own garden albeit down about fifteen stone steps. It also had a huge cellar that ran under the whole house. Peter saw incredible potential there, I saw a cold, dark cellar. He had plans to renovate it but we never did. It was great storage though!

My job at BUPA Murrayfield Hospital was going well and I really enjoyed the variety of work. Because it was a private hospital there were lots of different specialities which made it all interesting. Some I'd never experienced before like ophthalmic and orthopaedic surgery and also plastic surgery. There was even some paediatric nursing and as someone with a sick children's nursing qualification I often had responsibility for the children that came in. The staff were great and there were lots of incentives to work hard. We had corporate memberships to a gym, the zoo and various other activities. These were funded by donations from grateful patients and we had some incredible nights out also subsidised by their generosity. My colleagues were lovely, standards were high but we still had time to have a lot of laughs. It was there I met Helen Arnott and subsequently her husband Ronnie who would become surrogate grandparents to my children several years down the line. I also met my good friend Cecelia, another friendship that blossomed.

It was while I was working at BUPA that Dad died in October 1988, I was twenty six. Peter and I had gone on holiday to Corfu with his brother Roy. Definitely a different era looking back. We had no mobile phones and if you wanted to use the payphone in the village you had to queue up for over an hour. I had no reason to phone home and Dad still didn't have a phone in the house anyway and nor did I phone my siblings either. Dad was fit and healthy and only seventy two. He didn't even have a GP when he died, our family GP had retired about ten years previously and he had never re-registered with a new one! He died from a perforated duodenal ulcer which must have been painful and pretty frightening not to mention totally preventable. Liz had gone to see him, probably the day he died, but got no answer at the door. She didn't have a key; she'd never lived there. I know she suffered a lot after he died thinking if she'd only tried to get into the house she might have managed to save him. It's unlikely and the chances are he was already gone before she got there. We only have an approximate date of death for him but it could have been a day either side. The coroner had to rely on when neighbours and friends had last seen him. Because it was a sudden death there was a post mortem and so his funeral was delayed which worked well for me as I was back home in Edinburgh when I found out. Dad is buried with Mum in Greenacres Cemetery along with our maternal grandparents. I've often wondered since if he had had any wish to be taken back to Ireland but I'm guessing he would have wanted to stay with Mum.

My life continued in Edinburgh and after a couple of years, I thought I should make more use of my children's nursing qualification and reapplied to the "Sick Kid's Hospital" in Edinburgh. This time I got a job and started working on a medical ward. I really didn't like it and was thoroughly miserable for six months before going back to BUPA Murrayfield. I still had itchy feet though, and was trying to work out what I wanted to do with my career. Although I was glad to be back at BUPA, I was already hoping that at some point Peter and I would have children. I know plenty of people who have young children and work shifts but I really didn't want to. I began looking at how I could continue nursing and yet have more regular hours. I had enjoyed working in the community and started to think of Health Visiting as an option.

It was hard to get into Health Visiting, you had to apply for a place at college and to a health authority to fund you. Places were at a premium, especially for the funding. I applied to Lothian Health Board and Queen Margaret College. The first and second time I got the college place and no funding. The third time I applied to Fife Health Board for funding and got it...but not the college place! I had given my friend, Diane, from Booth Hall days, as one of my referees. She had resumed her Nursing Officer status and offered to phone the college on my behalf. The upshot was the college reconsidered and offered me a place and I was set to start my Health Visiting career. Because I was funded by Fife Health Board my placements would all be in Fife. I was lucky, I had two of the best mentors. Maureen Stirzaker in Dunfermline and Janet Cowie in Cowdenbeath. Janet in particular was fantastic. She taught me so much as did her colleagues Marjorie and Jean. Cowdenbeath is an old mining community and there was a lot of poverty. The people though were amazing, and Fife prided itself on "Caring for Kingdom." Unlike in some of the bigger cities, we visited families from cradle to grave. We had a remit to visit from when a baby was ten days old until they went to school. We also undertook "over 75 year old" health checks and visited vulnerable people on discharge from hospital as well as "at risk" families and individuals. I learned a lot and was sorry that when I finished the year training, there were no jobs in either Dunfermline or Cowdenbeath. Fife Health Board had funded my placement and one of the conditions was that they gave me a job at the end of the training and that I had to stay for a year. The job they offered was in Leven.

Leven is about an hour's drive from Edinburgh over the then Forth Road Bridge before the Caledonian Crossing was built. I wasn't overly happy about the commute, which I appreciate is quite normal for many people. I was based in Leven Health Centre with two separate GP practices. There were six Health Visitors in total, three for each practice. Three of us shared an office with the District Nurses who were also attached to the GP practice. In spite of my early misgivings, I loved it. Colleagues always make or break a job and my colleagues in Leven were exceptional. On my first day I was met by Frieda Irving. She was the Nursing Officer and my immediate boss. She was a kindly woman, not always effective or proactive but she absolutely had her staff's best interest at heart. She knew I hadn't wanted to come to Leven and just the fact she acknowledged it and made me welcome anyway made a difference.

I was taken into the office to meet my two Health Visiting colleagues, Pam and Ann. After introductions, they pointed to a huge filing cabinet and told me my "caseload" was in there but they were happy to help. They said I should stay in the office the first couple of days just to familiarise myself with what was there unless I had a "new baby" visit. I didn't, and so the two of them set out on their visits leaving me as the only Health Visitor on the premises. Leven was a mixed bag and took in the surrounding areas and villages. Ann had the very upmarket East Neuk of Fife on her caseload. Lots of farming families and business people – nightmare to cover when she was off as it was so hard to find the farms, no satnav then!

Pam had the other end of the spectrum and had a lot of vulnerable families, many living in poverty and often with the added concern of alcohol and drug misuse and child protection issues. My remit was Leven itself and a few outlying villages. For the most part my caseload was middle of the road although I did have some vulnerable families. More of that soon.

So, there I was, my first day thumbing through notes and feeling a bit overwhelmed with it all. Then I got a phone call from one of the receptionists to say there was a man downstairs who was looking for "lotion" – the receptionist was trying to be discreet but managed to convey she thought he had nits. She said she would ask the GP to write a prescription but I'd have to go and see to confirm it was indeed nits. I was delighted, something I could actually do. I'd seen plenty of nits during my training... and not always the insect variety!

I went downstairs with an air of confidence; the receptionist introduced me to the patient and found us a small consulting room. He was a youngish man, older than me, maybe early thirties. I was busy doing my best sympathetic, non-judgemental chat when I said, "Could you just let me see, so that I know which treatment to ask the doctor to prescribe please?" Without missing a beat, he dropped his trousers and said "It's crabs, I've had them loads of times, Dr Greenhough knows what lotion to give me." To say I was stunned was an understatement! Recovering quickly though I didn't have to look too close to see "the beasts" literally crawling around his nether regions! Ever the professional, I managed to stay calm and told him to get dressed while I got the prescription. The poor receptionist was mortified when I told her and promised me it wasn't a trick because I was new. It certainly broke the ice though and I felt very much part of the team from the start.

For the most part my caseload was interesting and the people of Leven, very welcoming. I did, however, have a few "at risk" families on my caseload and as a result had to give evidence in court on two occasions. One for a case of child abuse/neglect and the other a victim of domestic abuse. It was nerve wracking and I can only imagine how it felt for the women who were giving evidence against their partners. Pam, my colleague, seemed to be in court a lot as her caseload was a lot more volatile. She also had clients that she didn't see in their home, mostly because they were drug addicts and it would have been unsafe. Apart from the travelling which was tedious especially in the winter I loved my time in Leven.

It was while I was there, I got married!

19

Becoming Mrs Maxwell and a Mum

Peter and I got married in 1991 whilst I was working in Leven. We had been together nearly five years but in true Peter style it took him a long time to get round to it!

Our wedding day

Up to this point, Peter worked for British Gas. He had gone there from school at 15 and had worked all over Scotland converting homes to natural gas before we met. He was an Assistant Service Officer which was a middle management job based in Edinburgh. His brother Roy was the same grade although they worked in different depots. He and Roy also did "homers" at the weekend to earn extra money, something that helped enormously along with my extra nursing shifts when we were setting up the flat. It wasn't unusual for both of us to work seven-day weeks but we were young and didn't mind. Anyway, we had settled into an easy-going life, the flat was shaping up as we did renovations to it as often as we could afford to. It wasn't the most romantic of proposals although he did go down on one knee in the living room of the flat! We were married shortly after; we saw no reason to wait and neither of us wanted a big wedding. Peter thought we should get married in England and so I chose Manchester Town Hall. I phoned up to make all the arrangements, all was going smoothly until they asked where we lived. When I said Edinburgh, they told me one of us had to be resident in the area we were getting married in for six weeks prior to the wedding date. Obviously as we both had jobs in Edinburgh, that wasn't going to happen, we had to rethink fast. The last place I had lived before I moved north was Swinton in Salford. Fortunately, Penny still lived there and so when I contacted the registry office, I was ready with her address…we're still not really sure if we're actually officially married or not!

We honeymooned in Gran Canarias in a beautiful hotel, which was just as well since it rained for the whole of the second week! That's what happens when you get married in November. We hired a car though, and saw most of the island as we tried to outrun the rain.

We returned home to the news that British Gas was being restructured and Peter and Roy would have to reapply for their jobs. After several weeks of worry they both kept their grade but it meant travelling through to Glasgow every day, something Peter hated. Eventually he was offered a job in Central Heating Sales but his heart wasn't in it and when voluntary redundancy packages were on offer several months later, he took one. His few months in sales had paved the way for the next stage in his career…selling double glazing.

It was a bumpy start to married life as he didn't earn a salary, only commission and it seemed to be a feast or a famine. Fortunately, he and Roy still did "homers" occasionally and so we got by.

The year after we were married, Paul arrived. So, Peter now had three children, Michelle almost twenty-one, Stewart eighteen and a new baby. In those days, maternity leave wasn't overly generous and health visiting jobs were hard to come by. I was worried that if I gave up my job, I wouldn't get another and Peter's salary was commission based. I went back to work when Paul was three months old, taking him with me over to Leven to a wonderful childminder called Ann. She had three boys of her own, all teenagers and she was amazing. She let me go to her house at lunchtime to feed him and she brought him to my baby clinic in the health centre every week to get weighed, really just so I could see him. There was no doubt he was thriving and putting on weight. He was an easy baby. He ate and slept and smiled. He crawled early and was walking by nine and a half months...then the peace was shattered.

He was and still is a ball of vibrant energy, never stopping until bedtime. He was into everything, exploring cupboards and drawers, climbing everything above knee level and given his age and size, was as sure footed as a mountain goat!

Once we had Paul, we hoped we would have a second baby and knew the flat would be a tight squeeze. We had already converted the dining room into a nursery but knew eventually we would need to move. House prices had doubled since we bought the flat – great for selling ours but not so great for buying. We wanted to stay in and around Corstorphine Hill where we were but that proved to be out of the question in spite of our flat doubling in price from when we had bought it five years previously.

We saw our current home and this time I fell in love with it at first viewing. It needed a lot of cosmetic work but nothing on the scale that the flat had needed. One of the plusses was that it had a big enclosed back garden... somewhere we could contain Paul! We moved in when he was nine months old and have been here ever since, (at the time of writing in 2025).

It was around this time that a health visiting job came up in Edinburgh, fairly local to us in Blackhall, and so I applied and got it. Poor Ann was heartbroken, she had formed a lovely bond with Paul but our life was in Edinburgh and it was so much easier to get to work in fifteen minutes than an hour. We managed to find him a place at one of the Birrell Collection Nurseries in the grounds of the old Queen Margaret College where I had done my Health Visiting Diploma. It was a fantastic nursery and had some beautiful wide-open spaces with grass and flowers that the children played in. The staff were incredible and Paul transitioned really well, considering up to that point he'd only been with Ann and one other child that she looked after. The next few months were settled and I found out I was pregnant again.

Suzy was born in the autumn of 1994, although we didn't call her Suzy until she was several months old. She was always Suzanne in the beginning. Peter named her after a song from his favourite singer, Leonard Cohen and only realised later that it was about a lady of the night! It was only when she was about nine months old we shortened her name and she's been Suzy ever since. As for most young people with full time jobs and two small children, life was hectic. Both sets of grandparents had died long before Paul and Suzy were born and so we had no one around to help out. Peter's sister, Doreen, had two children older than ours but still young enough to need her and so although she was a great support she wasn't around in the same way grandparents can be. It was the same with my siblings who all had young children and they had the additional problem of being a couple of hundred miles away.

Suzy joined her brother at the Birrell Collection as again I returned back to work after three months. I was desperately looking for part time work but there was little around, even less than full time and so I had to carry on until she was about a year old when I got a part time liaison health visiting job based in a clinic in Edinburgh. Although I was based in the community my referrals came from the Western General Hospital in Edinburgh and I spent most mornings there rounding up discharge referrals from the Cardiac and Oncology units. I no longer visited young families and new babies and I did find the transition hard. It wasn't really what I wanted but I wanted the reduced hours and more time with my family and so it was well worth the trade-off.

Being a mum. The best job in the world!

20

Books and Reading

As I said, I read avidly throughout my childhood once I got going. Although I was such a bookworm, we had almost no books in the house. As I already mentioned the library was a home from home for me and I borrowed books at a phenomenal rate. I do remember Eric buying me an encyclopaedia/non-fiction book that I spent hours thumbing through looking at pictures from exotic places. One in particular was a giant tree, possibly a sequoia but I'm not sure. It was one of the few books that I actually owned, plus a fiction book called "Bob a Job Pony" which put me in a horse phase very briefly and for the only time in my life! As an adult I have totally overcompensated for my lack of books in childhood and have shelves full of them. It's almost an addiction but not one I want to recover from!

I loved all the Enid Blyton books, especially the adventures of the Famous Five, Secret Seven and Five Find Outers and Dog. My absolute favourites though were the Malory Towers and St Clare's books about boarding school life. I so wanted to go and be part of the whole midnight feast scene, no interest whatsoever in the education part of it! They were all very middle class, jolly hockey sticks types of books and were as far removed from my very working-class schools and background as possible. Still, that's what books do best, transport you to times and places that you otherwise wouldn't know about.

My favourite book of all time though is still The Secret Garden by Frances Hodges-Burnett and it's the book I go to now if I can't sleep. I can play it on audio from any given chapter and it doesn't matter when I drop off to sleep because I know it so well.

Unlike today, Young Adult (YA) wasn't a reading category and so you progressed from the children's section into adult books with little but the classics in between.

By the time I got to senior school I had made my way through almost all of Catherine Cookson's books – she was a Geordie who wrote family sagas. In my later teens I loved Stephen King and James Herbert novels and would scare myself silly with them. I wouldn't dream of reading a horror story now! I also read Jaws and watched the film, both of which are actually very tame, but in their day were seen as very scary. I never did read or watch the Exorcist, not after Eric said he couldn't have it in his bedroom at night when he was reading it! Again, by today's standards I believe it's very tame.

Books and reading have always been a source of pleasure and it was something I really wanted to instil in my children when they came along. I read to them literally while they were still in the womb. Bedtime stories were non-negotiable and I even read to them when they were in the bath. In recent years they've both said the bath-time stories were the best because they knew they were extra and didn't count as the bedtime story! They both loved stories. Paul enjoyed reading them less, and so in an attempt to keep his interest I got him a mini-Walkman cassette player. What a breakthrough, and just like Gran years before with the "Talking Books" it opened up a whole new world for him. We found out, when he was in Primary 5, that Paul is dyslexic, which made so much sense. I think it was a relief for him to know that finding reading tricky wasn't his fault. Now, he listens to audiobooks a lot and has been known to say that he's the best-read person that doesn't read!

When they were very young, we often felt like we had Thora Hird living with us. She was the actress who narrated the Alfie and Annie Rose stories, written by the legend Shirley Hughes. We met her a few times at the Edinburgh International Book Festival which was the highlight of our reading year. Alfie was later replaced by Harry Potter for

Suzy, and again we thought Stephen Fry might be living in the house or car because his voice was constantly reading in the background. Paul moved on quickly from Harry Potter but was mad about Terry Pratchett's, Truckers, Diggers and Wings and Carpet People and The Saga of Darren Shan by Darren Shan. He loved them all and it was as much a treat to buy a new audio as a new physical book for him. When we went on our long journeys down to England and France, they would plug themselves into their Walkmans, and later their personal CD players, and listen for almost the whole journey. Sometimes we would all listen to the same audiobook over the car stereo system but they could never agree on what, so mostly it was easier to keep the peace and let them listen on their own! Now of course technology has progressed so much and we just download to our phones, pop in the earphones and we're off. There was something magical though about the old cassette tapes and having to wind them back with a pencil to wherever you'd missed, or the CD's jumping when you walked or ran. We still felt we had the most up to date technology and I guess we did!

For many years as an adult, I read a lot of crime novels, mostly Scottish but also American and Canadian too. The only time we could persuade Peter to attend a literary event was when the crime writer, Ian Rankin, held a whisky tasting event along with a discussion of his latest book at the Edinburgh International Book Festival! The Edinburgh International Book Festival was the highlight of the year for me and Paul and Suzy and also Mags who often came up for it. One year, Mags and I got holed up in the Spiegel Tent because Ann Widdicombe, a Tory member of parliament, was at the festival and protesters were shouting and waving placards outside. We weren't allowed to leave in case we were accosted by the baying mob! Mostly though the Book Festival was a real literary treat for three whole weeks in August, blighted only by having to go back to school half way through. Imagine having the world's best book festival going on in your city and having to work through it! I'm sure there'll be many comments about teachers and holidays when this is read but I am thinking of the children too...honest!

I know that progress is essential and we can't hold on to the past but I do miss the Charlotte Square venue for its nostalgia and feel-good factor.

I've moved away from crime fiction as I've got older, not sure why because there's plenty of good stuff around. I do always return to it though if I'm in a reading rut or can't get into something else. I like the pace of crime fiction and many of its authors write a whole series. It's good to see how the characters develop and progress. My taste in reading is now very eclectic and I have surprised myself by enjoying some poetry, historical novels and some fantasy. I never really considered non-fiction to be reading, as such, but now I also read a lot of that too. Mostly it's about mindfulness and holistic therapies or the whoo whoo stuff or as Peter calls it the "snake oil" therapies! He remains my greatest reading challenge but then Peter, although undiagnosed, is almost certainly dyslexic. He has absolutely no interest in reading, other than an occasional newspaper, although one of my recent birthday gifts to him was a book of poems by Leonard Cohen, one of his favourite musicians and singers. He's read a few of those but he's definitely still not up for a novel, not even on audio. What surprises me is that for my birthday and Christmas he almost always buys me a book and rarely gets one that I don't like. I think there's a secret reader in there somewhere!

Friends From Near and Far

Peter and I didn't have a lot of friends in common when I first moved to Edinburgh. Although his split with his first wife wasn't particularly acrimonious, many of the "couples" he had been friends with, particularly the women, didn't seem to want a relationship with us. Peter was happy with his brother and other buddies from the pub and I had a good set of friends from work. There is also a twelve-year age gap between us which possibly played a part in us not having many "couple" friends in the early days, there were exceptions though.

My good friend from school, Angela Tunnacliffe, moved to California after completing her degree. She had spent a year in Santa Barbara during her course in American Studies and while there had met her future husband, Craig Sturgeon. I'd spent a lot of my later St. Anselm's years with Angela and was often invited to her house for dinner and sleepovers. Her mum made the most amazing Sunday dinners and I often thought if I had children, I wanted to be the kind of mum Irene is.

Peter and I went to California for a holiday and with Craig's help, managed to keep our visit a surprise from Angela! Again, just like with the Kuglers who I will speak about next, we have gone over to see them and they us, although on both counts, they've been here more than we've been there.

We did meet Angela and Craig in Florida one year when their children Bradley and Gemma were little more than babies. Paul and Suzy, who were around seven and five took them under their wings and Paul even taught Gemma, who wasn't even one how to catch a Pidgey on his GameBoy!

Although it sounds very old fashioned now, I had a penfriend who I had written to since my early teens. Suzanne lives in Portland, Oregon, USA. Our writing had waned a lot, mostly just Christmas and birthday cards. However, I did get a letter asking me if we would mind being a friendly contact for her brother-in-law and his wife, Mike and Cheryl Kugler, who were coming over to stay in Edinburgh for almost a year. Of course, we didn't mind and it was the start of a long friendship that we still have to this day. Mike was working on his PhD at the University of Edinburgh and Cheryl had given up her work to travel with him. We had some great times and it was a wonderful opportunity for us to do "touristy" things with them. We missed them a lot when they went back to Chicago but we did go over to visit them the following year when they had their first baby, Sarah. Over the years we have seen quite a bit of them. When Mike finished his PhD they moved to Iowa and we spent Easter with them there one year. Our kids went to the local school with Sarah and James for a couple of days and this was reciprocated when they came here to Edinburgh.

We've had some of the best times with the Kuglers and the Sturgeons in spite of the distances.

Closer to home we kept in touch with Penny (from my nursing days) and Shaun, who she did eventually marry but not for many years. When our children were younger, we would often meet in Ullswater, Cumbria and pitch up our tents for a weekend. We also met up with them abroad a couple of times. It was only as our kids reached mid-teens that we really grew apart and lost touch.

Bev from my nursing years has also been a constant in my life for decades now. We might not see each other, rarely more than once a year, but we just seem to pick up where we left off. I know I could phone any day of the week to Bev and she would come in a heartbeat if I needed her and I would do the same for her.

Just before I left BUPA Murrayfield a new nurse arrived. She was Maltese and full of fun and had moved from a hospital in London with her now husband, Derek. We became friends and still are to this day, having had children at similar times and our girls being in the same class for a few years in primary school. We have laughed together a lot and supported each other through life's ups and downs and more recently have taken up wild swimming together! Mostly, Cecelia likes to swim in the sea, as it reminds her of Malta. I'm not sure how the North Sea remotely compares with the Mediterranean Sea of her homeland but it does. More recently I've enjoyed swimming in Harlaw Reservoir and Linlithgow Lagoon with another friend Jane and a small group of her friends. Jane has been a neighbour for many years but we didn't become close until one of our other neighbours, Dolina, became ill. Dolina was an absolutely delightful lady who was in her nineties and still very much independent. She had a wicked sense of humour and had a very down to earth, no-nonsense approach to life. Before she died, she told both Jane and I that she was glad she had brought us together because we had so much in common, and we do. It's quite strange to think we have both trained in Reiki, Nordic Walking and enjoy many other similar activities. I was a nurse and health visitor and she was a midwife. We have lived across the road from each other for years but never knew each other well. We definitely became closer as we shared the grief of Dolina's illness and death, along with her daughter, Sheena.

One of my closest friends in recent years has been Irene. We were colleagues at Erskine Stewart's Melville Schools (ESMS) and have remained so in spite of her moving hundreds of miles from Edinburgh down to Devon. She is my go-to person for advice and is always so calm and measured too and…she does a pretty good job along with Angela Sturgeon in editing my books. Irene is very old school on the grammar and punctuation front and has a hard job whittling out my endless commas, semicolons and hyphens. Without the skills of these two wonderful friends and Angela's husband, Craig's IT skills my books would still be very unfinished and almost certainly not published.

FRIENDS FROM NEAR AND FAR

22

The Teaching Years

At school, I had often said I wanted to be a teacher, but when it came to career options and guidance there was very little of either. When I did talk about teaching, everyone said I would never get a job at the end of the training because there were too many teachers. This sounds ludicrous but was in fact a real problem in the late seventies. My brother Eric's wife at the time, Bev, had left a great job as a librarian to be a primary teacher but on completing the course struggled to get a job and ended up back at the library. I was easily persuaded in those days and quite fickle as we found out earlier going from a potential career in the police to nursing! All I can say in my defence is that, how are you supposed to know what you want to do for the rest of your life when you're only eighteen and never lived out of the town you were born in? Now, career pathways are completely different and it seems you can change and reinvent yourself many times over which can only be a good thing. Who would ever have thought then that being a nail technician, social media influencer, digital marketing assistant or data analyst would ever have been possible.

And so, I came to teaching in my mid-thirties. I applied to do the Post Graduate Certificate in Education (PGCE) at Moray House which is part of the University of Edinburgh. As with Health Visiting previously, you had to be accepted by both the university and a local authority which wasn't easy. On my third attempt I finally got the funding from Edinburgh and the University of Edinburgh and I started the year long course. Paul and Suzy were only six and four at the time and it wasn't an easy year on any front. Thankfully Peter, as always, was very supportive and was also working from home which made a huge difference to our childcare arrangements as he was around for drop off and pick up. It was very full on and pretty tough for all of us. Generally, I'm a morning person so having to study late into the evening/night wasn't great. I really had no choice though as the kids were up early and had to be breakfasted and sorted out for school and I had to be away on the bus to get across town. Early evenings were taken up with family life and organising for the next day so studying and lesson planning came much later in the evening after Paul and Suzy were in bed. I was very lucky that all my placements were in Edinburgh and actually quite local to our house. I had some great placements and some equally great mentors and I was able to complete the course.

When I finished the PGCE I managed to get a maternity cover job in the same primary school that Peter had gone to when he was a child. Broomhouse Primary had its challenges (even after Peter left!) but the staff were incredibly friendly and inclusive. I only had seventeen children in my first class and I never got to teach a class with those magic numbers again after that year! Sadly, for me the person I was covering returned from maternity leave and so I was back to looking for a job. I got one just a short distance away from Broomhouse in Hailesland Primary School which has since changed its name to Canal View Primary School. I job shared with a lovely lady who was very experienced and very generous when it came to mentoring me. Hailesland wasn't my favourite place though and I had already started my MSc in Professional Studies at University of Edinburgh part time focusing on Learning Difficulties as they were then known. When a Support for Learning job came up at Erskine Stewart's Melville Schools (ESMS) I applied and to my amazement got it. Not only that, but they agreed to finance the last year of my MSc!

There started a nineteen-year career in one of the best places I ever worked in.

23

The ESMS Years

I feel ESMS deserves a whole section to itself since I was there for so long! I started in 2003 in a part time role in the Support for Learning (SfL) department. I had been really concerned about applying for jobs in the state sector because they tended to have only one SfL teacher per school and it was quite daunting to think I might be responsible for organising and carrying out support to vulnerable children all by myself. I had the theory but didn't have any practical skills other than what I had picked up as a class teacher. It was very reassuring to be part of an experienced team of six plus an Educational Psychologist and I loved the work instantly. It had changed quite considerably by the time I left nineteen years later in 2022. I started out with small groups of mainly primary four and five children who were almost all dyslexic, although we had a smattering of children with what was then called dyspraxia as well as some speech and language difficulties. I only remember having concerns about one child who may have been on the autistic spectrum but that has changed significantly in recent years.

Collegiality at ESMS was second to none. I met some of the most talented and skilled teachers, many of whom have become lifelong friends.

As a part time member of staff there was no compulsion to be part of the vast extra-curricular programme but it was encouraged. I loved how there was so much choice and also funding to set up clubs. My love of reading kicked in and I started the Book Club which became very popular with the primary six and seven children and so I set up a Story Club for the primary fours and fives. Maggie Ferguson, the school librarian, was an inspiration and shared my love of books. The library had really taken off and Jane Hewitt, one of the Assistant Heads, Maggie and myself were given a remit to raise the profile of the library and reading in the school. It was the best project ever as far as we were concerned. Maggie had been involved a couple of times in the International Kids' Lit. Quiz hosted around the world by reading fanatic and Kiwi – Wayne Mills.

We decided to really go for it although most of the teams were from High schools not Primary schools. Any of the children could try out and we had many elimination rounds before choosing an A and a B team for the regional event. We went for several years and although we never won outright and didn't get to go to the finals in some of the exotic places, we did come second a couple of times and almost always beat our own Senior Schools from Stewart's Melville College and The Mary Erskine School, which was always a big bonus!

As a result of that I created the Lit. Quiz in school and every single class in the upper junior year groups took part against each other for four consecutive weeks. No mean feat for a school that had twenty-eight classes between primary four and primary seven. There was always great excitement on Friday afternoon when the results came out and the leaderboard went up. The teachers were as much invested in it as the children, so desperate were they for their class to be crowned Lit. Quiz Champions! It was a great way to get even reluctant readers to read and it was a real team/class effort as opposed to an individual event which would have been tough on the very children I taught in the SfL department.

I had also been going to yoga classes myself and had been interested in mindfulness for some time when I heard about a course to teach mindfulness and yoga to children. I approached the school and asked if they would fund the training and they agreed. That started me off on another extra-curricular adventure doing early morning yoga classes for the children and mindfulness meditation sessions for staff, before school. Many of the teachers were keen for me to have some input into their classes with mindfulness and Gill Douglas particularly was interested. Gill and I had started at ESMS on the same day as had Jane Hewitt who became Assistant Head and part of the legendary library team. Gill always welcomed me into her classroom and depending on what day we could both manage, my sessions with several of her classes became known as Mindful Mondays with Maxwell or Mid-week Mindfulness with Maxwell or just Mindfulness with Maxwell! Although we lost a bit of momentum over lockdown, we soon picked up again and I like to think those children I taught will have some strategies to use when life gets stressful.

The last three years at ESMS before I retired saw a slight change in my role. I had for several years worked predominantly with the primary seven-year group, so for children in Scotland that is the last year of primary school. Since ESMS takes children from nursery age right up to sixth form, I felt we had a unique opportunity to help our Junior School children transition to our two Senior Schools. The Junior School is co-ed but in Senior School the boys remained on the Stewart's Melville College (SMC) campus while the girls went to the Mary Erskine School (MES) about a mile up the road. This situation will change in 2026 when the Senior Schools will also become co-ed.

Anyway, when I broached this with the headmaster, he was all for it and so it seemed were the Governors too. I had wanted to reduce my hours prior to retiring and they were very accommodating, agreeing that I was to spend a day per week in the Junior School with the primary sevens and a day in each Senior School working with the S1 classes. My remit was mostly with those children who received Support for Learning, but also in the classroom situation and so I got to know many more children and teachers. I knew some of the Senior School teachers by virtue of being part of the school for so long but also because Paul and Suzy went to SMC and MES respectively. It was something different and I loved it; the teaching was second to none and I often said of the maths teachers that if only I had had input like this as a pupil, I would feel totally different about maths. I did learn a lot and am eternally grateful again for the shared knowledge and skills that I got from my colleagues and friends across the three schools.

All good things come to an end though...or do they? I was nostalgic but ready to retire from the "day job" in 2022 but I think ESMS is a place that gets under your skin and it's always hard to completely leave. I now invigilate for both Prelims in January and Scottish Qualification Authority (SQA) exams in May. I also had a brief sojourn on reception in 2024 which was good fun and so very nice to be back in school...for a short time.

24

Holidays With and Without Children

I feel very fortunate that throughout my life I have been able to go on holidays both to far flung destinations and those closer to home.

Holidays are always special times when you can relax and spend time together, and both as a couple and as a family, we have done that. Obviously, meeting Peter as a holiday romance changed my whole life too! Peter has always, probably more than me, wanted to go on holidays and I am so glad we did. Before we got married, we enjoyed a few holidays with Roy, Peter's elder brother, mostly to Corfu. Peter was close to Roy and was devastated when he died in 2002. He was his best friend as well as his brother and Roy was with him in Majorca when we met. Both of us have some lovely memories of our younger days in Kavos with Roy too. As with Magaluf, Kavos does have a bit of a reputation for partying but it wasn't like that for us...honest! What's hard to believe now though is that people smoked on planes! Roy was a heavy smoker and so opted for the smoking seats at the back of the plane. There was a curtain between the smokers and non-smokers which did absolutely nothing to keep the smoke away from us all up at the front of the plane. It was the same on buses and in pubs and an evening out almost always meant arriving home smelling like an ashtray. I don't miss those times and as I previously mentioned, apart from a couple of puffs of a Park Drive with Jennifer I have never had the urge to smoke.

In our early years together we also took Stewart, Peter's eldest son, camping in France a couple of times. I have some great memories of windsurfing (them) and canoeing (me), the latter very unsuccessfully and it's a sport I don't tend to embrace. I think it must be something to do with rolling the canoe and being submerged...not for me and definitely not in salty water! When Stewart turned eighteen, I was just about to have Paul and so we had to wait until he was born before we took them both to Florida. Great having a baby with you in Disney because they put you to the front of the queue and do a thing called "baby swap" so two of us got to go on a ride while the other held Paul and then we swapped so Stewart got lots of double rides!

We have never been on holiday with Michelle, Peter's eldest daughter, but have had some good times both in Aberdeen and Edinburgh as well as Dundee, the latter in lockdown for Peter's 70th birthday when all indoor gatherings were cancelled. We met in Camperdown Park and Michelle had even made him a birthday cake! There are lots of happy memories with both the Halls and the Maxwells, especially get-togethers at our house with them all together including our lovely grandchildren: Kailyn, Adam, Dan, Greg and Charlotte.

Holidays have always been special to us and before Paul was born, we bought a trailer tent and often went down to the Lake District for weekends. After he and Suzy were born, we took them camping in France, the Netherlands and Spain. We had some fantastic EuroCamp holidays too which were more luxurious than the trailer, having a fridge and camp beds. One place in the Pyrenees had ponies on site and Paul was always sneaking out of the Kids Club to visit them until one bit him! Duinrell, in the Netherlands was another favourite place of ours when the kids were young. Duinrell is a campsite and mini theme/water park which was just perfect for us. The rides and water park were all free for campers and as with most campsites it meant the children got a lot of freedom to wander around with new friends and old.

Duinrell was only a short train journey to Amsterdam and we spent some happy times sightseeing there visiting Anne Frank's house and queuing for ages to see Van Gogh's Starry Night painting when Paul was learning to play Don McLean's version on guitar. We waited for ages to get in the gallery only to find that the painting was on loan and in New York...we never did see it!

We also met the same Irish family three years running in France and they even came to see us when they were in Edinburgh. Sadly, we lost touch after a few years but we are still in touch with two of our oldest friends Liz and Peter Watkins. We met when we took the trailer tent just after Paul's first birthday to St Georges de Didonne in Royan on the west coast of France. We hit it off with Peter and Liz immediately and after that often stayed overnight with them in Waring before getting on the overnight ferry to St. Malo on subsequent camping holidays.

When Paul was doing his "van tour" around Europe, many years later he stayed with them in Spain, where they had moved, for a couple of weeks. Peter and Liz looked after him really well and also reassured us that he was fine when we hadn't heard from him for a while!

We also met up with Bev and her husband, my friend from Salford Royal nursing days on the same campsite the same year which would have been 1993, since Paul had just had his first birthday.

We were lucky enough to take Paul and Suzy to Walt Disney World, Florida three times and to Disneyland in California once. One of the Florida trips was to Adventure Cove where we swam with dolphins, a magical experience. On one of our Florida trips, we met up with Angela and Craig and their two children, Bradley and Gemma who are younger than Paul and Suzy. Our last time in Florida was just after Paul's eighteenth birthday and it was different but equally fun to be with two (adult?!) children. We still did the parks but we also did water skiing, a boat trip and saw things differently than when they were younger. We of course did the whole Harry Potter (HP) experience at Universal Studios since Suzy was and still is a diehard HP fan!

As Paul and Suzy got older, they of course went off on their own holidays and trips. Paul did a lot with scouts both in the UK and also in Europe and he has enjoyed snowboarding in Slovakia too. Suzy did a whole trip to Asia on her own, and has danced all over the world in Europe, China, Russia as well as the UK.

We were lucky enough to go and watch Suzy dance in Moscow when she took part in the Spasskaya Tower Military Tattoo. What an experience. Peter, Paul and Georgie (Paul's soon-to-be wife in 2025!) along with Doreen and Davie, Peter's sister and brother-in-law, went over the weekend. We packed as much as we possibly could into that trip, including a boat ride up the river, a tour of the underground stations which are beautifully decorated, as well as of course watching Suzy dance in the tattoo. What a beautiful place Moscow is and we're so glad to have been able to see it.

One of the best things about having adult children is that sometimes they still agree to go on holiday with "the parents!" We've been lucky enough to go away at Christmas several times with them as adults. We've mostly been to Lanzarote and once to Tenerife and I think, as a parent, it's a real privilege to spend time away with your adult children.

In 2018, Peter and I went on a Baltic cruise - what an experience! For me the best part was waking up each morning in a different country. We visited all the capital cities of the Scandinavian countries as well as Tallin in Estonia, Warnemunde in Germany and St Petersburg in Russia. Growing up, these were places I could only dream of visiting and I feel so fortunate to have visited them. The following year we did a tour of South Africa and again, I feel extremely lucky to have seen this fabulous country, wildlife and culture for ourselves. We also crossed over the border into Eswatini which is the former Swaziland.

Some of mine and Peter's other trips, closer to home, have been Portugal, which is a beautiful country with a breathtaking coastline, Frankfurt, Prague and Budapest. Both Frankfurt and Budapest were with Doreen and Davie, Frankfurt for Peter's sixtieth birthday. It's hard to believe that it will be fifteen years ago this year at the time of writing (2025). How fast time goes.

In recent years, while I was still working and Davie couldn't travel, Peter and Doreen went away together to both Portugal and Lanzarote.

I was lucky enough to go to Rome with my sister Liz, ten years ago, and we did all the sights during a very short, hot, February half term. Mags and I along with Peter and Robert have had some lovely short breaks too, in and around Scotland. One of the best was up to Oban and over to Tobermory on the ferry.

Visits to my good friend Irene in Totnes, Devon have become annual events and have given me a chance to see a part of the country I wasn't familiar with. It's also good to relax, walk and gossip – definitely "girls only" time!

Holidays are definitely a way to recharge your batteries although admittedly sometimes getting there and back can be stressful. They are a time for chilling out, taking stock of what's going on in our lives and spending quality time with friends and family. Here's to many more happy holidays with those near and dear to me.

25

Writing

Writing has been part of my life now for well over a decade. I had started writing the odd short story but had no idea what I was doing until I started a writing class in 2011 at Tynecastle High School in Edinburgh. I signed up for it not knowing what to expect. It was a mixed group, some had been writing for years, others like me complete novices. The teacher, Jane, had a lovely manner. She was very encouraging, knowledgeable and inclusive; the classes, interesting and fun. When the course came to an end there wasn't a follow-on class but we could sign up and repeat the same one again. A few of us decided we would maybe just meet up ourselves and encourage each other and four of us still do! Sue, Georgia, Stephen and I have been meeting regularly since then and have shared many pleasant hours both reading each other's pieces and writing on the "hoof."

I have also ventured into several other writing groups, the majority not regularly. In the early days after Jane's class, Sue and I decided to go to a writer's group in a little book/coffee shop in Edinburgh. What an experience, what a laugh…but we didn't repeat it! It was predominantly men, in fact Sue and I were the only women apart from the "Chair." The men were an "eclectic" mix - a songwriter, a novelist, short story writers (none of which were short). There were a lot of Sci-Fi enthusiasts and a lot of "zapping" and "kerpows" in their stories. When I tentatively asked one of them, who claimed his writing was a children's novel, if he thought parents would be happy to buy it with all the swear words in it, he was very unrepentant and told me,

"My grandson's eleven and loves it, no I'm leaving the F*** words in!"

It went on for almost three hours because they all had to read everything they had, no filter, no five hundred-thousand words each that we were restricted to in Jane's class and no two stars and a wish either. The latter was Jane's way of making criticism constructive, two nice comments and one suggestion for improvement. Sue and I quickly learned there was no need for improvement in any of their minds, their writing was perfect just as it was! At ten pm we escaped and found the nearest pub where we laughed till our sides ached and had a much-needed drink. We never went back!

While in Jane's class at Tynecastle I started a novel which sounds very grand but it's still not finished and I think now with hindsight it needs to be rewritten as opposed to edited! During lockdown we got a kitten, Luna, and because I was furloughed for part of the time, I wrote a few short picture book stories about her and her adventures for younger children. I incorporated some mindfulness into them and sent them off to publishers and agents. I had absolutely no luck, and it's no consolation really when people tell you that some of the best authors have countless rejections before getting a book deal…I'm still waiting! I decided though that as a retirement/sixtieth birthday present to myself that I would publish my first Luna book through what is known as a vanity publisher. This basically means you pay them to publish your book but they do all the hard work like layout and in my case found and commissioned an illustrator. There is something quite amazing about seeing what you have written published as a book. Luna's First Garden Adventure was indeed a lovely gift to myself but I couldn't afford to do the rest in the same way. I also had the idea of writing a handbook for teachers on how to teach mindfulness in the classroom since I wasn't able to do it in person anymore. I took a different route with this one and self-published it with a lot of help from good friends. A best seller it isn't but I still get a kick out of seeing my name in print and hope it helps teachers somewhere to introduce some mindfulness into their classrooms. My latest self-publication is another picture book about Luna – Luna and the Cat Flap. I have been going into schools and reading both Luna books and incorporating mindfulness techniques too. I love reading to the younger age groups although when I was teaching, I preferred older children. So far, I have read my books in about ten different schools in Edinburgh, one in Devon and also online to schools in Leeds and Canada!

Writing is definitely something I want to do regularly and of course I have written my memoir which you are reading right now! I'm sure anyone who doesn't have a connection to the times, places and people I'm writing about won't have any interest but I've enjoyed doing it. I hope someone at least finds it interesting and can relate to some of the themes I've explored. If not, it doesn't matter, it's been an interesting experience and a reminder of people, places and times I had forgotten.

It's not going to make the New York Times Bestseller list but I'm happy to have written it.

Epilogue

So, here it is. The story of my life from being born in 1962 to being sixty-two years old. The whole purpose of writing this is so that Paul and Suzy have some kind of record of the English and Irish side of their family. Being the youngest of four, by nine years, and my mum dying when I was fourteen months old has meant that my life has taken a different course than that of my siblings. The age gap for me between my siblings is also reflected in the age gap between Paul and Suzy and their cousins. Unfortunately for them, Paul and Suzy have never known their true grandparents on either side of the family although there have been several excellent substitutes for them. I didn't even live with my brothers except for the year I was born as they were so much older than me. As a child, my sisters were like surrogate mothers although that changed significantly once I became an adult and they became my friends as well as sisters. Their memories are so different to mine, particularly Mags' because she had Mum for twelve years before she died and then in many ways as the eldest girl, was expected to fulfil that role for dad and the boys. She was at "home" with them while Liz and I were at Gran's.

I don't expect this to be of too much interest to either of my children yet, not for a while at least, if at all. I do think it's a good idea to have the information written somewhere just in case they are interested at some point though. I found out the hard way when I started writing that a lot of the people who could give me answers aren't around because we have lost touch or they have died. As my good friend Irene, who edited a lot of this book for me says, "Reading this is like a piece of history." And it is!

Life has changed so much over the last six decades it's only when I started to write this, I realised just how much. Culturally, environmentally, socially and in so many other different ways the world has changed. This brings to mind the line from my favourite poem, Desiderata by Max Ehrman.

"And whether or not it is clear to you, no doubt the universe is unfolding as it should."

Eric once bought Gran a copy of this and it was up on her wall throughout my childhood and I loved it. I have added the whole poem at the end just so you can read it all. Even though it was written many years before I was born, it still seems full of good advice even today.

So, whoever you are and whenever you read this, I hope it will shed some light on a life and family that you may or may not be a part of. Even so, I'd like to think it gives some idea of what it was like to live in a different era. Although life was often tough, I don't necessarily think it was tougher than life is now. In many ways life was simpler, expectations lower and emotional and physical resilience key to how we lived. Challenges for this generation now (2025) and beyond are so different. That doesn't mean they aren't just as important and it's hard to compare the incomparable. Generally, though, people have always wanted the same things. To be happy and loved, to have a purpose in life, a home and enough food and the odd luxuries and comforts to keep us going. Those things mean different things to different people and generations but I don't think any of us can go far wrong if we stick to the advice in the Desiderata poem along with another favourite line of mine from my yoga class. Although I have no one to credit this to I think it's a nice quote to finish on!

"Be kind whenever you can but most importantly be kind to yourself."

Desiderata
(Latin: Desired things)

Go placidly amid the noise and the haste, and remember what peace there may be in silence. As far as possible, without surrender, be on good terms with all persons.

Speak your truth quietly and clearly; and listen to others, even to the dull and the ignorant; they too have their story.

Avoid loud and aggressive persons; they are vexatious to the spirit. If you compare yourself with others, you may become vain or bitter, for always there will be greater and lesser persons than yourself.

Enjoy your achievements as well as your plans. Keep interested in your own career, however humble; it is a real possession in the changing fortunes of time.

Exercise caution in your business affairs, for the world is full of trickery. But let this not blind you to what virtue there is; many persons strive for high ideals, and everywhere life is full of heroism.

Be yourself. Especially do not feign affection. Neither be cynical about love; for in the face of all aridity and disenchantment, it is as perennial as the grass.

Take kindly the counsel of the years, gracefully surrendering the things of youth.

Nurture strength of spirit to shield you in sudden misfortune. But do not distress yourself with dark imaginings. Many fears are born of fatigue and loneliness.

Beyond a wholesome discipline, be gentle with yourself. You are a child of the universe no less than the trees and the stars; you have a right to be here.

And whether or not it is clear to you, no doubt the universe is unfolding as it should. Therefore, be at peace with God, whatever you conceive Him to be. And whatever your labours and aspirations, in the noisy confusion of life, keep peace in your soul. With all its sham, drudgery and broken dreams, it is still a beautiful world. Be cheerful. Strive to be happy.
by Max Ehrmann ©1927

Acknowledgements

Huge thanks to Angela Sturgeon and Irene Williams for their patience and editing skills. Also, Craig Sturgeon for his amazing IT skills.

Thank you all, this wouldn't be in print without you.

Thank you to Peter for his unswerving support and for Paul and Suzy just for being who you are!

In Memory

**Mum and Dad,
Mary and
Jim Fitzimons**

**My Gran, Sarah
Winterbottom**

www.ingramcontent.com/pod-product-compliance
Lightning Source LLC
Chambersburg PA
CBHW071246070526
44583CB00017B/2347